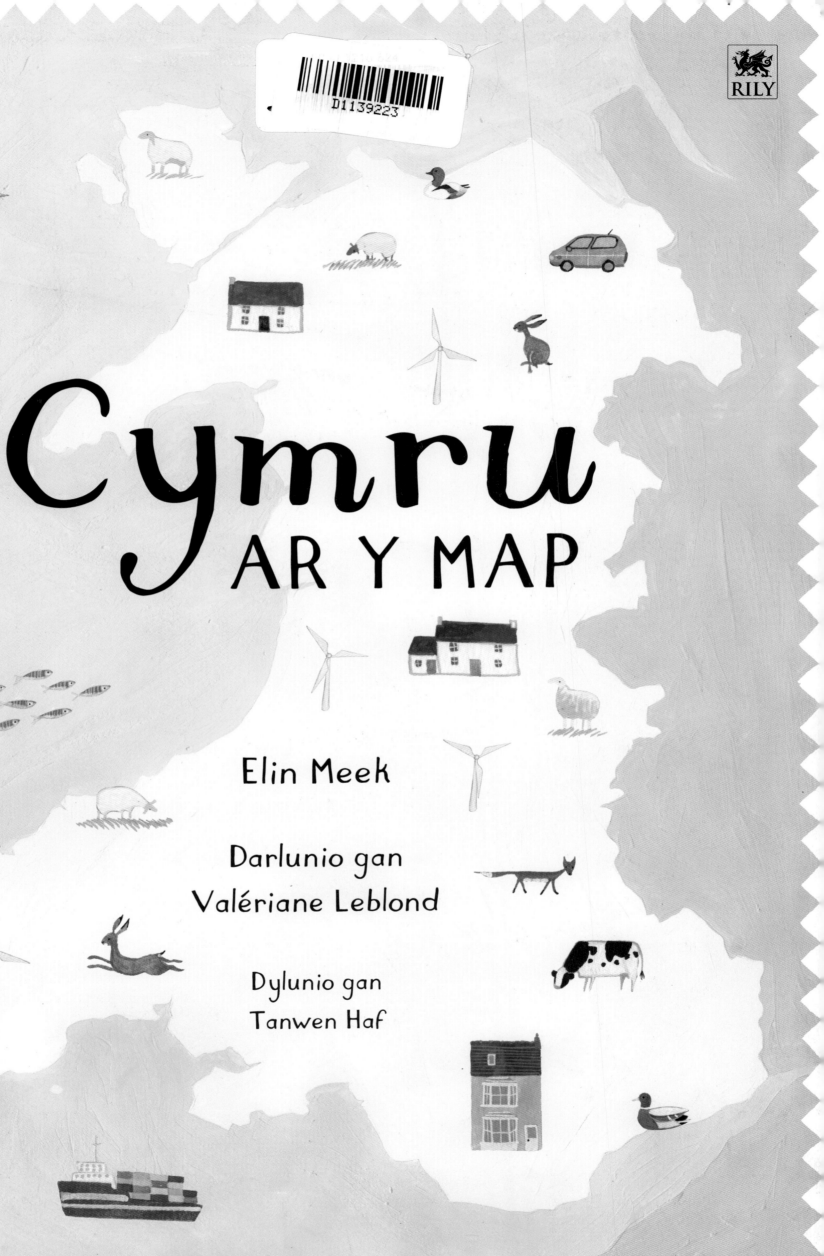

Cymru
AR Y MAP

Elin Meek

Darlunio gan
Valériane Leblond

Dylunio gan
Tanwen Haf

D1139223

RILY

I Matthew, a ddaeth â fi i Gymru,
ac i Wyre, Alban a Nebo.
Cymru — gwlad fy meibion.
— Valériane Leblond

Cymru oedd 'Gwlad fy Mam', ac mae'r llyfr hwn
yn gyflwynedig i'r anhygoel, y galonogol a'r eithriadol
Mairwen Thomas, ac i bob un o'n mamau rhyfeddol.
— LT, Rily

Cymru
AR Y MAP

Cyhoeddwyd gan Rily Publications Ltd 2018
Rily Publications Ltd, Blwch Post 257, Caerffili CF83 9FL
Hawlfraint © Rily Publications Ltd 2018

ISBN 978-1-84967-054-8

Hawlfraint y testun © Elin Meek, 2018
Hawlfraint y darluniau © Valériane Leblond, 2018

Dylunwyd y ffontiau gan Valériane Leblond a Tanwen Haf.

Cyhoeddwyd gyda chymorth ariannol Cyngor Llyfrau Cymru.

Cedwir pob hawl. Ni chaniateir atgynhyrchu unrhyw ran o'r cyhoeddiad hwn na'i gadw
mewn cyfundrefn adferadwy na'i drosglwyddo mewn unrhyw ddull, na thrwy unrhyw
gyfrwng electronig, nac fel arall, heb ganiatâd ymlaen llaw gan y cyhoeddwyr.

Argraffwyd yn China.

Llyfrgelloedd Sir Y Fflint
Flintshire Libraries
6824

SYS
WJ 912.429   **£12.99**

HO

rily.co.uk

CYNNWYS

YNYS MÔN
4–5

CONWY
10–11

SIR Y
FFLINT
14–15

SIR
DDINBYCH
12–13

WRECSAM
16–17

GWYNEDD
(ARFON A DWYFOR)
6–7

GWYNEDD
(MEIRIONNYDD)
8–9

POWYS
(SIR DREFALDWYN)
20–21

CEREDIGION
18–19

POWYS
(YR HEN FAESYFED
A BRYCHEINIOG)
22–23

TORFAEN
45

SIR BENFRO
24–25

SIR GAERFYRDDIN
26–27

MERTHYR
TUDFUL
38–39

BLAENAU
GWENT
44

SIR
FYNWY
48–49

CASTELL–NEDD
PORT TALBOT
30–31

ABERTAWE
28–29

RHONDDA
CYNON TAF
36–37

CAERFFILI
42–43

CAERDYDD
40–41

CASNEWYDD
46–47

PEN–Y–BONT
AR OGWR
32–33

BRO
MORGANNWG
34–35

FFEITHIAU

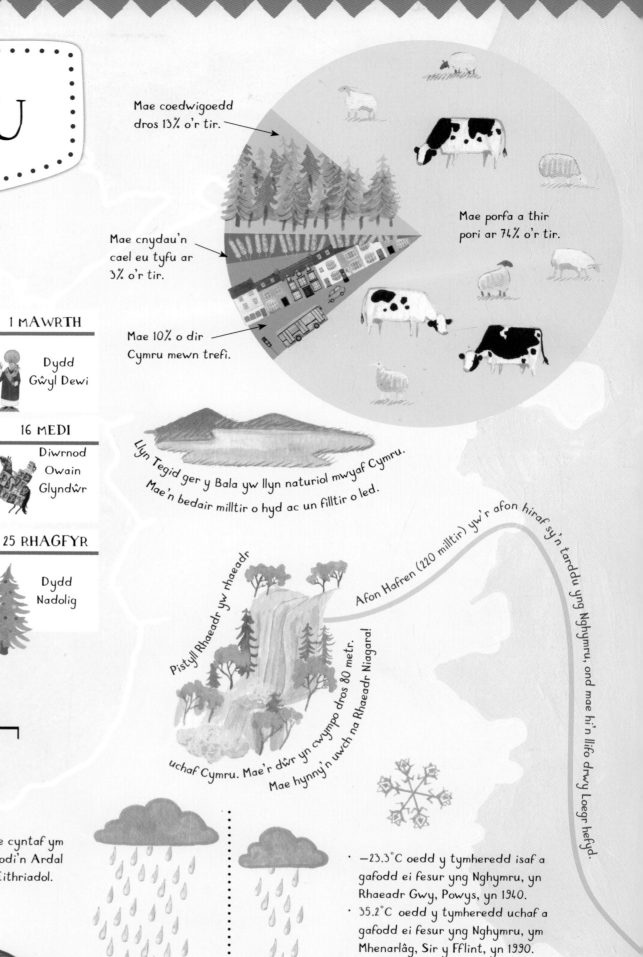

Mae coedwigoedd dros 13% o'r tir.

Mae porfa a thir pori ar 74% o'r tir.

Mae cnydau'n cael eu tyfu ar 3% o'r tir.

Mae 10% o dir Cymru mewn trefi.

DYDDIADAU PWYSIG

1 IONAWR	13 IONAWR	25 IONAWR	1 MAWRTH
Dydd Calan	Yr Hen Galan, sy'n cael ei ddathlu yn Sir Benfro	Gŵyl Santes Dwynwen, Santes Cariadon Cymru	Dydd Gŵyl Dewi
MAI	**GORFFENNAF**	**AWST**	**16 MEDI**
Eisteddfod yr Urdd	Sioe Amaethyddol Frenhinol Cymru	Yr Eisteddfod Genedlaethol	Diwrnod Owain Glyndŵr
15 HYDREF	**31 HYDREF**	**11 RHAGFYR**	**25 RHAGFYR**
Diwrnod Shwmae Sumae	Nos Galan Gaeaf	Dydd Llywelyn ein Llyw Olaf — Y Cymro olaf i fod yn Dywysog Cymru	Dydd Nadolig

Shwmae

Sumae

Llyn Tegid ger y Bala yw llyn naturiol mwyaf Cymru. Mae'n bedair milltir o hyd ac un filltir o led.

Afon Hafren (220 milltir) yw'r afon hiraf sy'n tarddu yng Nghymru, ond mae hi'n llifo drwy Loegr hefyd.

Parciau Cenedlaethol Cymru
Mae tri pharc cenedlaethol yng Nghymru ers:

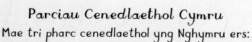

1951 — Eryri

1952 — Parc Arfordirol Sir Benfro

1956, 1957 — Bannau Brycheiniog

Mae'r parciau'n cynnwys 20% o arwynebedd Cymru gyfan.

Penrhyn Gŵyr oedd y lle cyntaf ym Mhrydain i gael ei ddynodi'n Ardal o Harddwch Naturiol Eithriadol.

Pistyll Rhaeadr yw rhaeadr uchaf Cymru. Mae'r dŵr yn cwympo dros 80 metr. Mae hynny'n uwch na Rhaeadr Niagara!

· −23.3°C oedd y tymheredd isaf a gafodd ei fesur yng Nghymru, yn Rhaeadr Gwy, Powys, yn 1940.
· 35.2°C oedd y tymheredd uchaf a gafodd ei fesur yng Nghymru, ym Mhenarlâg, Sir y Fflint, yn 1990.

Y wisg Gymreig sy'n cael ei gwisgo ar Ddydd Gŵyl Dewi

· het ddu
· betgwn
· ffedog
· siôl
· crys rygbi Cymru
· cap stabl

· Mae gorllewin Cymru'n cael 40% yn fwy o law na'r dwyrain.
· Mynydd Crib Goch, Gwynedd, sydd â'r record am y glawiad mwyaf mewn mis ym Mhrydain — 1396.4mm ym mis Rhagfyr 2015.

Cymru yw un o'r gwledydd gwlypaf yn Ewrop.

Mae mwy o gestyll y milltir sgwâr yng Nghymru nag yn unrhyw wlad arall — roedd tua 600 yn arfer bod, ac mae 100 ar ôl heddiw!

CYMRU AM BYTH!

Arwyddair
"Cymru am Byth!"

Mae'r rhan fwyaf o dir Cymru dros 150 metr o uchder.

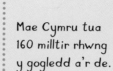

Yr Wyddfa (1,085 metr) yw mynydd uchaf Cymru.

Yng Nghonwy mae canran uchaf y bobl dros 65 oed (25%).

8,000 milltir sgwâr yw arwynebedd Cymru.

Mae Cymru tua 160 milltir rhwng y gogledd a'r de.

Yn Wrecsam mae canran uchaf y plant rhwng 0 a 5 oed (7%).

Teithio

· Y Rhufeiniaid adeiladodd y ffyrdd cyntaf yng Nghymru.
· Mae Llywodraeth Cymru'n gofalu am draffordd yr M4, sy'n 75 milltir o hyd, a 1,000 o filltiroedd o briffyrdd eraill. Y cynghorau sir sy'n gofalu am y gweddill.
· Cafodd y rheilffyrdd cyntaf eu hadeiladu i gludo glo i'r porthladdoedd.
· Mae rheilffyrdd Cymru yn aml yn dilyn yr arfordir, er mwyn osgoi'r mynyddoedd.

· Mae 26% o boblogaeth Cymru'n byw mewn ardaloedd trefol.
· Mae 20% o boblogaeth Cymru'n byw mewn pentrefi lle mae llai na 1,500 o bobl yn byw.

Mae tua 5,000 o bobl yn siarad Cymraeg ym Mhatagonia, yr Ariannin, lle'r aeth ymfudwyr o Gymru yn y 19eg ganrif.

Y Gymraeg

· Mae 20% o boblogaeth Cymru'n dweud eu bod nhw'n gallu siarad Cymraeg. Mae'r ganran uchaf (65%) yng Ngwynedd, a'r ganran isaf (8%) ym Mlaenau Gwent.
· Mae 23% o ddisgyblion Cymru'n mynd i ysgolion cyfrwng Cymraeg.

Mae arfordir Cymru'n 1370 milltir o hyd. Gallwch gerdded Llwybr Arfordir Cymru, sy'n 870 milltir o hyd.

Ieithoedd swyddogol Cymru yw

Cymraeg   a   Saesneg.

Mae Cymru rhwng 60 milltir a 124 milltir o led o'r dwyrain i'r gorllewin.

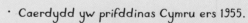

· Caerdydd yw prifddinas Cymru ers 1955.
· Tyddewi yn Sir Benfro yw'r ddinas leiaf ym Mhrydain. 2,000 o bobl sy'n byw yma.
· Yn Llanelwy, mae bron i 3,500 o bobl yn byw.
· Mae Abertawe yn ddinas ers 1969. Hi yw'r unig ddinas yng Nghymru sydd heb eglwys gadeiriol.
· Mae Bangor yn ddinas ers y 6ed ganrif.
· Casnewydd yw dinas fwyaf newydd Cymru. Mae'n ddinas ers 2002.

Mae 6 Safle Treftadaeth y Byd UNESCO yng Nghymru. Allwch chi chwilio amdanyn nhw yn y llyfr hwn?

· Mae bron i dair miliwn o bobl yn byw yng Nghymru (2,910,200).
· Mae 75% o boblogaeth Cymru'n byw yn ne-ddwyrain y wlad.

Llywodraeth

· Mae Cynulliad Cenedlaethol gan Gymru ers 1998.
· Adeilad y Senedd ym Mae Caerdydd yw cartre'r Cynulliad.
· Mae 60 o Aelodau Cynulliad.

3

Ynys Môn

714 km² (276 milltir²)

Cafodd George North, y chwaraewr rygbi, ei fagu ar Ynys Môn.

Melin Llynnon (1775) yw'r unig felin wynt yng Nghymru sy'n dal i weithio.

BAE CEMAES

LLYN ALAW

• Llanddeusant

Roedd Ynys Môn yn arfer cynhyrchu digon o rawn i fwydo Gymru gyfan, felly roedd yn cael ei galw'n 'Môn, Mam Cymru'.

Ynys Arw •

Goleudy Ynys Lawd •

Caergybi •

Mae llongau'n hwylio oddi yma i Ddulyn a Dún Laoghaire yn Iwerddon.

AFON ALAW

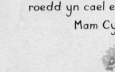

Dyma le gwych i weld adar y môr, ar ôl mynd i lawr 400 o risiau!

YNYS GYBI

BAE TREARDDUR

Cafodd Osian Roberts, un o hyfforddwyr tîm pêl-droed Cymru, ei fagu ym Modffordd.

Sw Môr Môn yw acwariwm mwyaf Cymru.

i Gaerdydd

Mae tua 1,200 o longddrylliadau o gwmpas yr ynys ac mae deifwyr yn hoffi mynd i'w gweld.

Mae adfeilion Llys Rhosyr, hen lys Llywelyn ab Iorwerth o'r 13^{eg} ganrif, i'w gweld yma.

Yma mae adfeilion Eglwys Santes Dwynwen, santes cariadon Cymru.

Ynys Llanddwyn •

MAE LLWYBR ARFORDIR MÔN YN 125 MILLTIR (200KM) O HYD.

• Amlwch

Roedd gwaith copr ar Fynydd Parys am ganrifoedd. Heddiw, mae'r tir yn goch fel y Blaned Mawrth, gyda chraterau fel y lleuad.

Mae cofeb yma i Richard Evans (1905–2001), llywiwr bad achub RNLI Moelfre. Mae'n un o 5 o bobl yn unig sydd wedi ennill gwobr aur RNLI, a hynny am achub 281 o fywydau.

YNYS MÔN
POBLOGAETH TUA
69,700
★ ★ ★

Moelfre •

MYNYDD BODAFON

Gerllaw Moelfre digwyddodd llongddrylliad y *Royal Charter*, un o longddrylliadau gwaethaf Prydain yn y 19eg ganrif. Boddodd 452 o bobl.

Ynys Seiriol

TRAETH COCH

LLYN CEFNI

Mae gwaith Syr Kyffin Williams a Charles Tunnicliffe, dau artist o Fôn, i'w weld yn Oriel Ynys Môn.

Castell Biwmares (o 1295) yw castell olaf a chryfaf Edward I yng Nghymru. Mae'n safle Treftadaeth y Byd.

Bodffordd •

Llangefni •

LLANFAIRPWLLGWYNGYLLGOGERYCHWYRNDROBWLLLLANTYSILIOGOGOGOCH

Biwmares • ★
🏰 CASTELL

Dyma'r enw lle hiraf yn Ewrop, ond Llanfair PG yw'r fersiwn byr!

Llanfairpwllgwyngyll gogerychwyrndrobwll llantysiliogogogoch

Porthaethwy •

Mae **Pont y Borth** (1826), gan Thomas Telford, yn 417m o hyd. Cyn i'r bont gael ei hadeiladu, roedd fferi'n croesi Afon Menai.

Pont Britannia

GWYNEDD

Brynsiencyn •

• Niwbwrch

Mae pâr o lewod calchfaen ar y ddau ben i **Bont Britannia** gan Robert Stephenson (1850). Dyma rigwm y Bardd Cocos (John Evans o Borthaethwy) amdanyn nhw:

Pedwar llew tew
Heb ddim blew:
Dau'r ochr yma
A dau'r ochr drew.

AFON MENAI

Mae Pili Palas yn gartref i bilipalod, pryfed ac anifeiliaid eraill.

5

GWYNEDD

2,548 km² (984 milltir²)

ARFON A DWYFOR

Mae llawer o bobl yn dweud mai Caernarfon yw tref Gymreiciaf Cymru.

Mae castell Edward I (1296) yn safle Treftadaeth y Byd.

ARFON

POBLOGAETH TUA

61,500

DWYFOR

POBLOGAETH TUA

28,100

Yn Llandwrog mae stiwdio recordio Sain, y cwmni recordio annibynnol Cymraeg cyntaf. Y canwr Dafydd Iwan oedd un o'r sylfaenwyr yn 1969.

BAE CAERNARFON

Mae gwenithfaen o chwarel Trefor yn cael ei ddefnyddio i wneud meini cwrlo.

• Trefor

Nant Gwrtheyrn •

Hen bentref chwarel wenithfaen, sydd nawr yn ganolfan dysgu Cymraeg.

Bu David Lloyd George, Prif Weinidog Prydain rhwng 1916 ac 1922, yn byw yma. Mae cofgolofn iddo ar y Maes yng nghanol Caernarfon.

Gallwch groesi'r swnt ar gwch o Borth Meudwy, ger Aberdaron, i Ynys Enlli. Yn ôl y chwedl, mae 20,000 o saint wedi'u claddu yno.

LLWYBR ARFORDIR CYMRU

Llanystumdwy

PENRHYN LLŶN

Plas Heli yw cartref yr Academi Hwylio Genedlaethol.

Pwllheli •

Aberdaron •

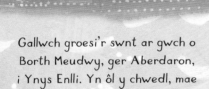

Aber-soch •

Pentref glan môr poblogaidd.

YNYS TUDWAL FAWR

YNYS ENLLI

Sefydlodd Deiniol Sant fynachlog ym Mangor yn y 6ed ganrif. Mae eglwys gadeiriol a phrifysgol yma.

Bangor

Sefydlodd y Rhufeiniaid gaer Segontium yma tua OC 78.

Y Felinheli

Roedd llechi o Chwarel Dinorwig yn cael eu hallforio o'r cei yma yn y 19eg ganrif. Mae marina yma heddiw.

Bethesda

GWYNEDD
POBLOGAETH TUA
123,600
★ ★ ★

Caernarfon
CASTELL 🏰 ★

Mynydd uchaf Cymru, 1,085m o uchder. Mae sawl llwybr yn arwain i'r copa, neu gallwch fynd ar y trên bach o Lanberis.

CARNEDD LLYWELYN

Pentref pwysig yn ardal y chwareli. Heddiw gallwch chi hedfan ar weiren sip dros hen Chwarel y Penrhyn, lle mae'r cerflun 'Dathlu'r Llechen Las'.

Llanberis

CASTELL DOLBADARN

Llandwrog

YR WYDDFA

GLYDER FAWR

Cododd Llywelyn ab Iorwerth y castell tua 1230.

Mae Amgueddfa Lechi Cymru yn Llanberis.

ERYRI

Mae Lili'r Wyddfa'n tyfu yn Eryri, yr ardal lle mae mynyddoedd uchaf Cymru. Dyma'r unig fan ym Mhrydain lle mae hi'n tyfu.

DWYFOR

Beddgelert

Gallwch fynd o dan ddaear i weld hen fwynglawdd copr Sygyn.

Blaenau Ffestiniog

Cricieth

CASTELL

Porthmadog

AFON GLASLYN

AFON DWYRYD

MEIRIONNYDD

CONWY

BAE TREMADOG

PARC CENEDLAETHOL ERYRI

Un o gestyll Llywelyn ab Iorwerth (1230au).

Roedd llechi Ffestiniog yn arfer cael eu hallforio o Borthmadog. Gallwch fynd ar drên stêm oddi yma i Flaenau Ffestiniog neu i Gaernarfon.

7

Blaenau Ffestiniog

MEIRIONNYDD
POBLOGAETH TUA
34,000

Portmeirion

AFON DWYRYD

MOELWYN
MAWR

Maentwrog

Pentref Eidalaidd a gafodd ei
godi rhwng 1925 ac 1976 gan y
pensaer Clough Williams-Ellis.

LLYN
TRAWSFYNYDD

Roedd Plas Tan y Bwlch yn gartref i'r
teulu Oakeley, perchnogion y chwareli
llechi ym Mlaenau Ffestiniog.
Nawr gallwch astudio'r
amgylchedd yma.

Trawsfynydd

Harlech ★
CASTELL ▮

Un o gestyll Edward I (1289)
sy'n safle Treftadaeth y
Byd. Daeth Owain Glyndŵr
i reoli'r castell yn 1404 ac yna
cynhaliodd ei ail senedd yma
yn 1405.

RHINOG
FAWR

RHINOG
FACH

COED-Y-BRENIN

Cafodd Hedd Wyn o fferm
Yr Ysgwrn, Trawsfynydd ei
ladd mewn brwydr ar ddiwedd
y Rhyfel Byd Cyntaf, cyn cael
gwybod iddo ennill cadair yr
Eisteddfod Genedlaethol.

PARC
CENEDLAETHOL

**Abermo/
Bermo**

AFON MAWDDACH

Porthladd pwysig i allforio gwlân,
llechi a phlwm yn y 18^{fed} a'r
19^{eg} ganrif. Mae'n dref wyliau
glan môr heddiw.

Dechreuodd
Llywelyn ab Iorwerth
godi'r castell
tua 1221.

Dolgellau

**CADAIR
IDRIS**

ARFORDIR CYMRU

LLWYBR

Mae'r awdures
Manon Steffan Ros
yn byw yn ardal
Tywyn.

**CASTELL
Y BERE** ▮

Llanfihangel-y-Pennant

AFON DYSYNNI

Gallwch deithio ar
reilffordd Tal-y-llyn o
Dywyn i Nant Gwernol.

Mae cofgolofn yma i Mary Jones, a gerddodd
tua 28 milltir (45km) i'r Bala yn 1800 pan oedd
hi'n 15 oed i brynu Beibl gan Thomas Charles.

Tywyn

BAE CEREDIGION

Porthladd prysur lle roedd
llongau'n cael eu hadeiladu yn y
19^{eg} ganrif. Mae twristiaid yn heidio
yma heddiw.

Aberdyfi

AFON DYFI

8

CEREDIGION

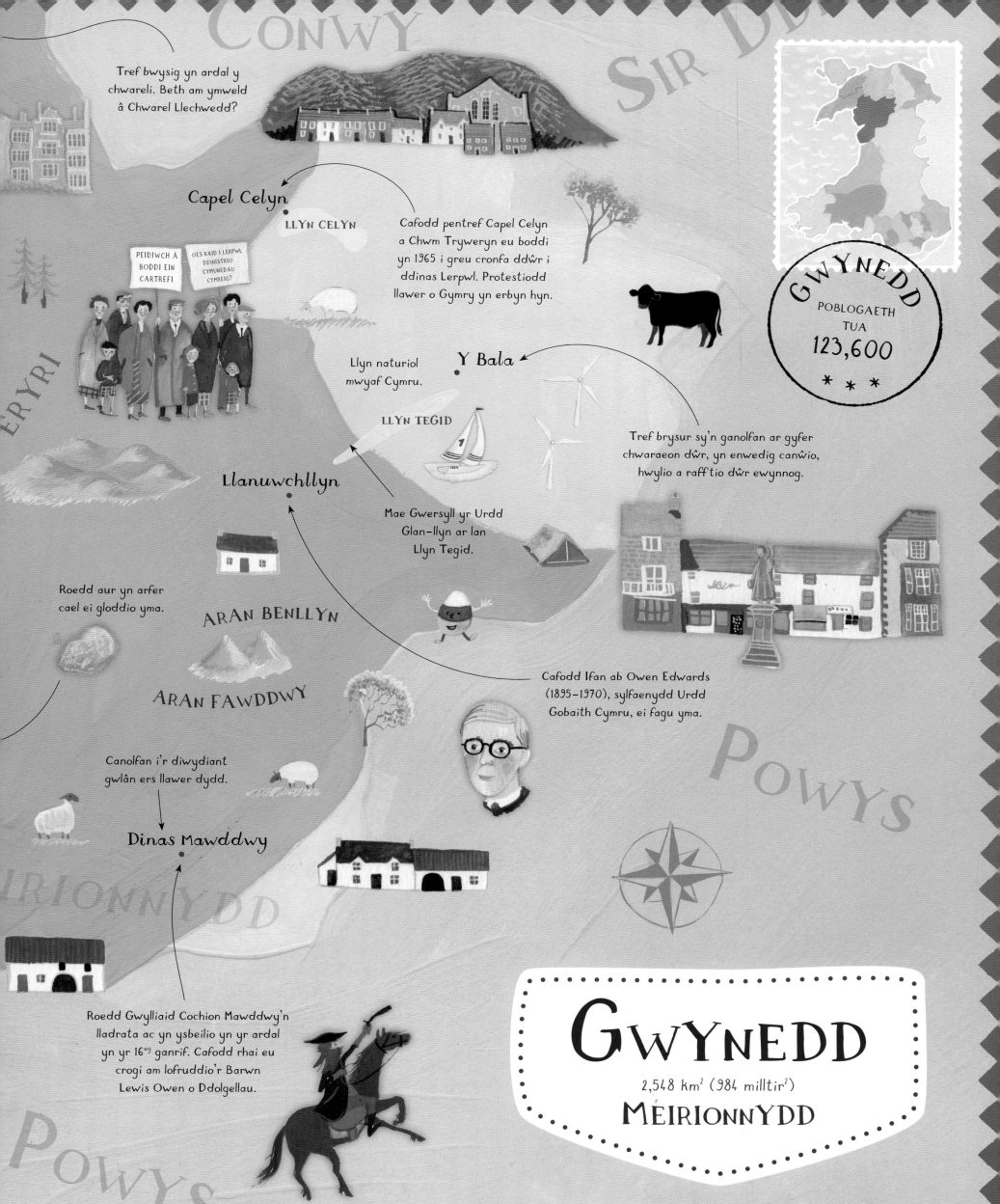

Tref bwysig yn ardal y chwareli. Beth am ymweld â Chwarel Llechwedd?

Capel Celyn

LLYN CELYN

PEIDIWCH Â BODDI EIN CARTREFI

OES RAID I LERPWL DDINISTRIO CYMUNEDAU CYMREIG?

Cafodd pentref Capel Celyn a Chwm Tryweryn eu boddi yn 1965 i greu cronfa ddŵr i ddinas Lerpwl. Protestiodd llawer o Gymry yn erbyn hyn.

Llyn naturiol mwyaf Cymru.

Y Bala

LLYN TEGID

Tref brysur sy'n ganolfan ar gyfer chwaraeon dŵr, yn enwedig canŵio, hwylio a raff'tio dŵr ewynnog.

Llanuwchllyn

Mae Gwersyll yr Urdd Glan-llyn ar lan Llyn Tegid.

Roedd aur yn arfer cael ei gloddio yma.

ARAN BENLLYN

ARAN FAWDDWY

Cafodd Ifan ab Owen Edwards (1895–1970), sylfaenydd Urdd Gobaith Cymru, ei fagu yma.

Canolfan i'r diwydiant gwlân ers llawer dydd.

Dinas Mawddwy

Roedd Gwylliaid Cochion Mawddwy'n lladrata ac yn ysbeilio yn yr ardal yn yr 16^{eg} ganrif. Cafodd rhai eu crogi am lofruddio'r Barwn Lewis Owen o Ddolgellau.

GWYNEDD POBLOGAETH TUA 123,600 ★ ★ ★

GWYNEDD

2,548 km² (984 milltir²)

MEIRIONNYDD

MÔN

GWYNEDD

Mae twristiaid wrth eu boddau'n cerdded ar hyd promenâd Llandudno.

Mae'n debyg mai'r bwthyn hwn ar y cei yng Nghonwy yw'r tŷ lleiaf ym Mhrydain.

Gallwch gerdded, mynd yn y car, mewn tram neu gar cebl i Benygogarth.

Llandudno

CASTELL DEGANWY

Bae Colwyn

CASTELL Conwy ★

Cyffordd Llandudno

Penmaen-mawr

Gardd Bodnant

Mae castell Conwy'n un o gestyll Edward I a gafodd ei gwblhau yn 1287. Mae'n safle Treftadaeth y Byd.

Mae pontydd enwog o'r 19eg ganrif yng Nghonwy – pont grog Thomas Telford, a phontydd rheilffordd Robert Stephenson.

Mae Conwy'n un o'r trefi caerog canoloesol gorau ym Mhrydain.

Mae gwarchodfa'r RSPB ar lannau aber afon Conwy. Mae'n lle gwych i weld pob math o adar, ym mhob tymor.

DYFFRYN CONWY

Trefriw

LLYN CRAFNANT

Llanrwst

PARC CENEDLAETHOL ERYRI

Capel Curig

Betws-y-coed

Plas y Brenin yw'r Ganolfan Fynydd Genedlaethol.

MOEL SIABOD

Mae ymwelwyr yn dod yma ers oes Victoria i weld y Rhaeadr Ewynnol.

CASTELL

Dolwyddelan

Mae castell Dolwyddelan yn un o gestyll tywysogion Gwynedd. Mae'n debyg i Llywelyn ab Iorwerth (Llywelyn Fawr) gael ei eni yma yn 1173.

AFON CONWY

LLYWELYN AB IORWERTH

10

LLWYBR ARFORDIR CYMRU

Tywyn

Abergele

Beth am fynd i weld pob math o anifeiliaid gwyllt yn Sw Mynydd Cymru?

Digwyddodd llifogydd difrifol yn Nhywyn yn 1990. Roedd rhaid i filoedd o bobl adael eu cartrefi. Mae'r morglawdd wedi cael ei wella ers hynny.

SIR DDINBYCH

SIR Y FFLINT

CONWY
POBLOGAETH
TUA
116,500
★ ★ ★

Llanfair Talhaearn

• Llansannan

Cewch weld nwyddau gwlân yn cael eu gwneud ym melin wlân Trefriw.

Mae pont hardd Llanrwst o'r 17^{eg} ganrif yn debyg i siâp bwa. (Dydy gyrrwr yn un pen iddi ddim yn gallu gweld cerbyd yn y pen arall.)

Digwyddodd damwain reilffordd waethaf Cymru yma yn 1868. Lladdwyd 33 o bobl.

Mae twristiaid yn heidio i arfordir Conwy yn yr haf.

LLYN BRENIG

LLYN ALWEN

entrefoelas

Ydych chi'n meddwl bod y Tŷ Hyll yn hyll?

Cerrigydrudion

Roedd ceffylau'r goets fawr yn arfer cael eu newid yma, ar ffordd yr A5 rhwng Llundain a Chaergybi. Thomas Telford gododd y ffordd. Roedd rhai teithwyr yn hwylio draw i Iwerddon wedyn.

NEDD

SIR DDINBYCH

CONWY
1,130 km² (440 milltir²)

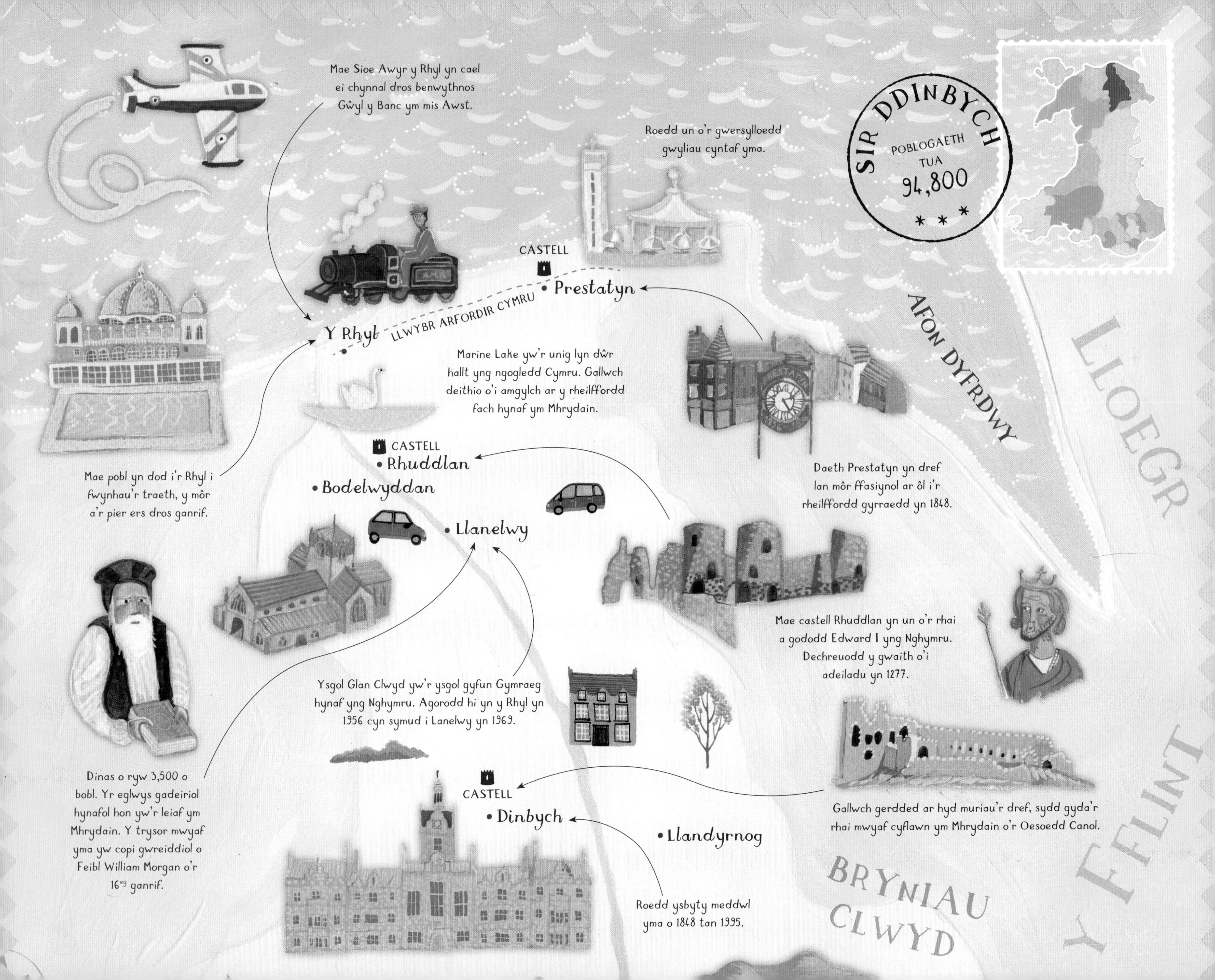

SIR DDINBYCH
POBLOGAETH TUA 94,800
★ ★
★ ★

BRYNIAU CLWYD

AFON DYFRDWY

Roedd un o'r gwersylloedd gwyliau cyntaf yma.

Daeth Prestatyn yn dref lan môr ffasiynol ar ôl i'r rheilffordd gyrraedd yn 1848.

Mae castell Rhuddlan yn un o'r rhai a gododd Edward I yng Nghymru. Dechreuodd y gwaith o'i adeiladu yn 1277.

Gallwch gerdded ar hyd muriau'r dref, sydd gyda'r rhai mwyaf cyflawn ym Mhrydain o'r Oesoedd Canol.

CASTELL
• Prestatyn

Marine Lake yw'r unig lyn dŵr hallt yng ngogledd Cymru. Gallwch deithio o'i amgylch ar y rheilffordd fach hynaf ym Mhrydain.

Y Rhyl — LLWYBR ARFORDIR CYMRU

CASTELL
• Rhuddlan

• Bodelwyddan

• Llanelwy

• Llandyrnog

Roedd ysbyty meddwl yma o 1848 tan 1995.

CASTELL
• Dinbych

Mae Sioe Awyr y Rhyl yn cael ei chynnal dros benwythnos Gŵyl y Banc ym mis Awst.

Ysgol Glan Clwyd yw'r ysgol gyfun Gymraeg hynaf yng Nghymru. Agorodd hi yn y Rhyl yn 1956 cyn symud i Lanelwy yn 1969.

Mae pobl yn dod i'r Rhyl i fwynhau'r traeth, y môr a'r pier ers dros ganrif.

Dinas o ryw 3,500 o bobl. Yr eglwys gadeiriol hynafol hon yw'r leiaf ym Mhrydain. Y trysor mwyaf yma yw copi gwreiddiol o Feibl William Morgan o'r 16^{eg} ganrif.

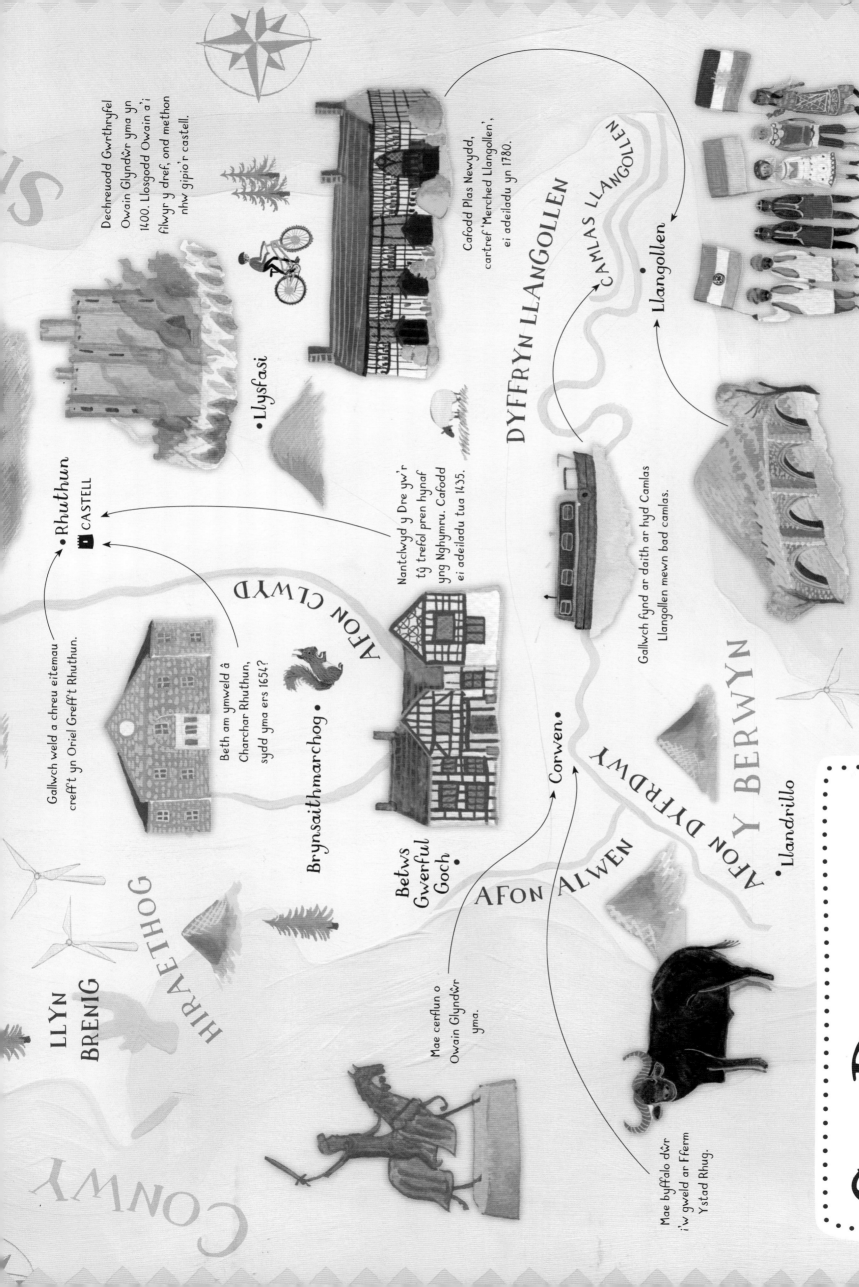

Dechreuodd Gwrthryfel Owain Glyndŵr yma yn 1400. Llosgodd Owain a'i filwyr y dref, ond methon nhw gipio'r castell.

Cafodd Plas Newydd, cartref 'Merched Llangollen', ei adeiladu yn 1780.

CAMLAS LLANGOLLEN

DYFFRYN LLANGOLLEN

Llangollen

Bob blwyddyn, mae pobl o bedwar ban y byd yn dod i Eisteddfod Ryngwladol Llangollen yn ystod wythnos gyntaf mis Gorffennaf.

•Llysfasi

Nantclwyd y Dre yw'r tŷ trefol pren hynaf yng Nghymru. Cafodd ei adeiladu tua 1435.

Gallwch fynd ar daith ar hyd Camlas Llangollen mewn bad camlas.

Roedd pont Llangollen yn un o hen Saith Rhyfeddod Cymru.

•Rhuthun ◼ CASTELL

AFON CLWYD

Gallwch weld a chreu eitemau crefft yn Oriel Crefft Rhuthun.

Beth am ymweld â Charchar Rhuthun, sydd yma ers 1654?

Brynsaithmarchog •

AFON Y BERWYN

Betws Gwerful Goch •

Corwen•

AFON DYFRDWY

•Llandrillo

AFON ALWEN

Mae cerflun o Owain Glyndŵr yma.

LLYN BRENIG

HIRAETHOG

Mae byffalo dŵr i'w gweld ar Fferm Ystad Rhug.

SIR DDINBYCH
844 km² (326 milltir²)

SIR Y FFLINT

169 km² (438 milltir²)

LLOEGR

SIR Y FFLINT

POBLOGAETH TUA
154,400

* * *

Mae'r llawr sglefrio yng Nghanolfan Hamdden Glannau Dyfrdwy yn gartref i Ganolfan Chwaraeon Iâ Cymru.

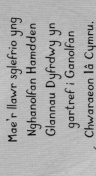

Mae pererinion yn dod i Ffynnon Santes Gwenffrewi ers OC 660. Maen nhw'n credu bod y dŵr yn gallu gwella pobl.

Cododd Edward I gastell yma rhwng 1277 ac 1285.

Y Fflint • 🏰 CASTELL

CEG AFON DYFRDWY

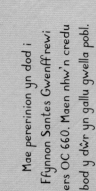

• Treffynnon

MYNYDD HELYGAIN

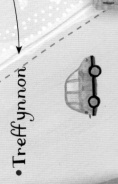

• Mostyn

GOLEUDY TALACRE

Y Parlwr Du

Roedd un o byllau glo dwfn olaf Cymru yma. Cafodd ei gau yn 1996.

Mae porthladd yma ers dros fil o flynyddoedd. Cafodd ei wneud yn fwy yn yr 21ain ganrif, fel bod llongau mawr yn gallu angori yma.

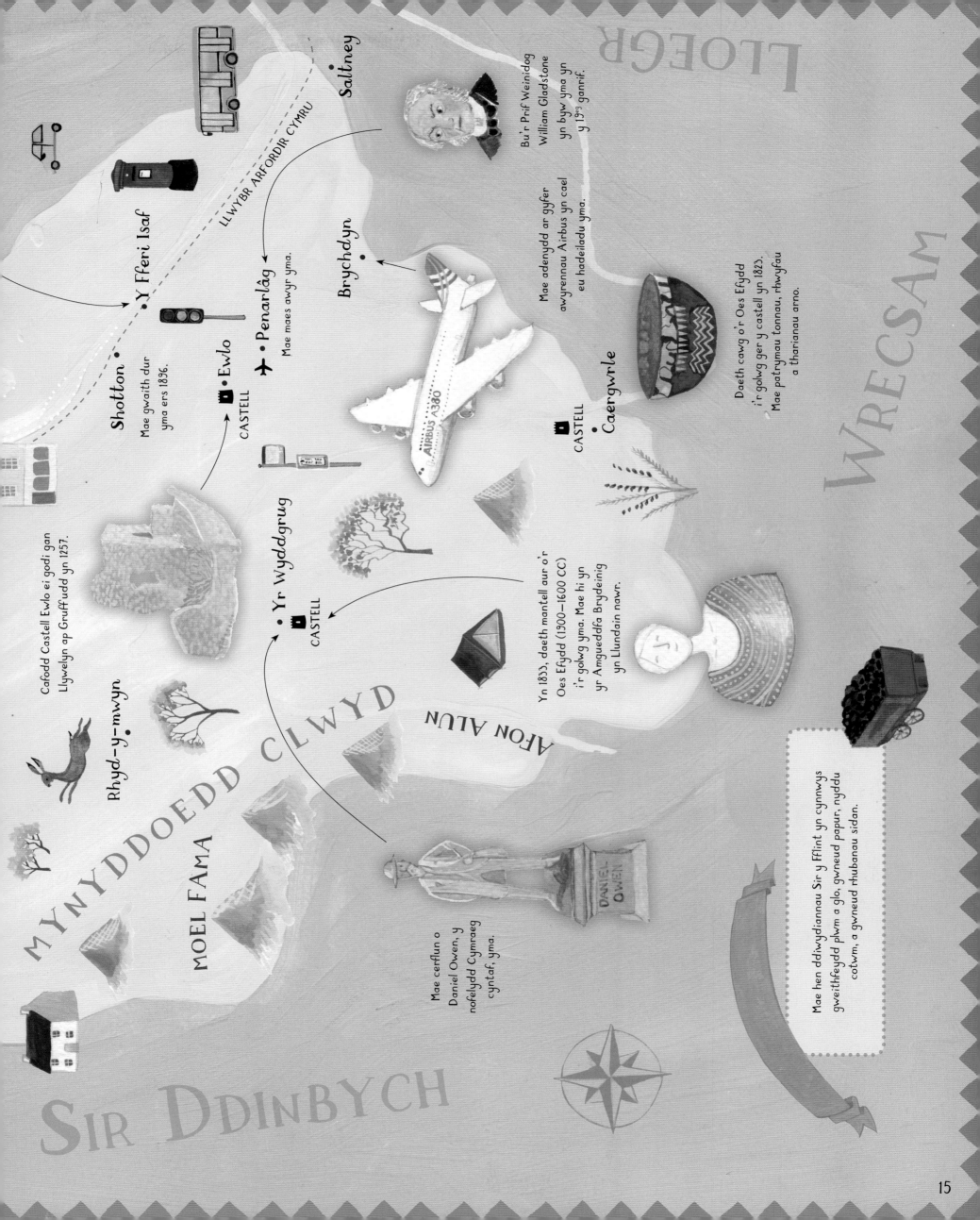

WRECSAM

Saltney

Bu'r Prif Weinidog William Gladstone yn byw yma yn y 19^{eg} ganrif.

Mae adenydd ar gyfer awyrennau Airbus yn cael eu hadeiladu yma.

Brychdyn

Daeth cawg o'r Oes Efydd i'r golwg ger y castell yn 1823. Mae patrymau tonnau, rhwyfau a tharianau arno.

Y Fferi Isaf

LLWYBR ARFORDIR CYMRU

Shotton

Mae gwaith dur yma ers 1896.

Penarlâg
Mae maes awyr yma.

Ewlo
CASTELL

AIRBUS A380

Caergwrle
CASTELL

Cafodd Castell Ewlo ei godi gan Llywelyn ap Gruffudd yn 1257.

Yr Wyddgrug
CASTELL

Yn 1833, daeth mantell aur o'r Oes Efydd (1900–1600 CC) i'r golwg yma. Mae hi yn yr Amgueddfa Brydeinig yn Llundain nawr.

Rhyd-y-mwyn

MYNYDDOEDD CLWYD

MOEL FAMA

AFON ALUN

Mae cerflun o Daniel Owen, y nofelydd Cymraeg cyntaf, yma.

DANIEL OWEN

Mae hen ddiwydiannau Sir y Fflint yn cynnwys gweithfeydd plwm a glo, gwneud papur, nyddu cotwm, a gwneud rhubanau sidan.

SIR DDINBYCH

15

WRECSAM

499 km² (193 milltir²)

Mae'r Stiwt yn ganolfan
gelfyddydau sy'n gartref
i gwmni theatr ieuenctid.

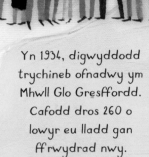

Yn 1934, digwyddodd
trychineb ofnadwy ym
Mhwll Glo Gresffordd.
Cafodd dros 260 o
lowyr eu lladd gan
ffrwydrad nwy.

Mae Llŷr Williams,
y pianydd byd-enwog,
yn dod o'r Rhos.

Rhosllannerchrugog
(y Rhos)

Pentref glofaol
oedd y Rhos
yn wreiddiol.

AFON DYFRDWY

Rhiwabon •

Mae Traphont Pontcysyllte yn
Safle Treftadaeth y Byd. Cafodd
ei chodi gan Thomas Telford a
William Jessop. Ers 1805, mae'n
cludo camlas 39m uwchben afon
Dyfrdwy. Gallwch gerdded dros
y draphont ar lwybr tynnu,
neu fynd ar gwch.

★ Traphont
Pontcysyllte

Glyn Ceiriog
•

AFON CEIRIOG

Y Waun
↑

Roedd chwareli
llechi'n arfer bod yma.

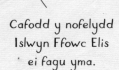

Llanarmon
Dyffryn
Ceiriog

Cafodd y nofelydd
Islwyn Ffowc Elis
ei fagu yma.

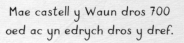

Mae castell y Waun dros 700
oed ac yn edrych dros y dref.

SIR Y FFL

SIR DDINBYCH

POWYS

POW

Roedd clychau eglwys y plwyf yn un o Saith Rhyfeddod Cymru.

AFON ALUN

WRECSAM
POBLOGAETH
TUA
136,700
★★★

• Gresffordd

CASTELL 🏰
Holt •

Cafodd clwb pêl-droed Wrecsam ei sefydlu yn 1864.

Cewch ddysgu am wyddoniaeth yn Techniquest Glyndŵr.

WRECSAM

Mae eglwys St Giles yn un o Saith Rhyfeddod Cymru. Mae'r tŵr i'w weld am filltiroedd.

• Erddig

Gallwch ymweld â thŷ a gerddi Erddig, un o blastai gorau Prydain. Cafodd ei godi rhwng 1684 ac 1687.

• Owrtyn

Roedd Rhiwabon yn enwog am haearn, glo a chemegau. Mae teils a brics yn dal i gael eu cynhyrchu yma.

Hanmer

Roedd 21 hen ywen Owrtyn yn un o Saith Rhyfeddod Cymru.

GWESTY'R WYNNSTAY ARMS, WRECSAM

Mae'n debyg mai yng ngwesty'r Wynnstay yma y cafodd Cymdeithas Bêl-droed Cymru ei sefydlu yn 1876. Ond mae gwesty'r Wynnstay yn Wrecsam yn honni hynny hefyd!

GWESTY'R WYNNSTAY ARMS, RHIWABON

CEREDIGION

688 km² (1,783 milltir²)

Llyfrgell Genedlaethol Cymru yw llyfrgell fwyaf Cymru. Mae'n cadw copi o bob llyfr a chylchgrawn sy'n cael eu cyhoeddi ym Mhrydain. Mae mapiau, ffotograffau a llawysgrifau pwysig yma hefyd.

Gallwch fynd ar daith i weld dolffiniaid a llamhidyddion ym Mae Ceredigion.

BAE CEREDIGION

Beth am fwynhau hufen iâ mêl yn y dref glan môr liwgar hon?

→ Aberaeron

Llanerchaeron

Ceinewydd •

Roedd llongau'n cael eu hadeiladu yma yn y 19^{eg} ganrif. Mae twristiaid yn heidio yma heddiw.

Ynys Aberteifi •

Llangrannog •

 LLWYBR ARFORDIR CYMRU

• Aber-porth

Yn y 19^{eg} a'r 20^{fed} ganrif, roedd yn ganolfan bwysig ar gyfer adeiladu llongau a physgota. Heddiw, mae maes awyr a chanolfan feteorolegol yma.

Ydych chi wedi bod yng Ngwersyll yr Urdd a'r Ganolfan Sgio yma?

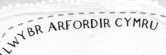

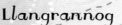

• Aberteifi
▉ CASTELL

Yn 1176 cynhaliodd yr Arglwydd Rhys yr eisteddfod gyntaf yn y castell hwn. Roedd y dref yn arfer bod yn ganolfan adeiladu llongau ac yn borthladd pwysig.

John Nash (1752–1835), y pensaer, gynlluniodd blas Llanerchaeron tua 1794. Aeth ymlaen i gynllunio Palas Buckingham a Regent Street yn Llundain a Phafiliwn Brighton. Gallwch chi ymweld â'r plas a'r fferm.

SIR BENFRO

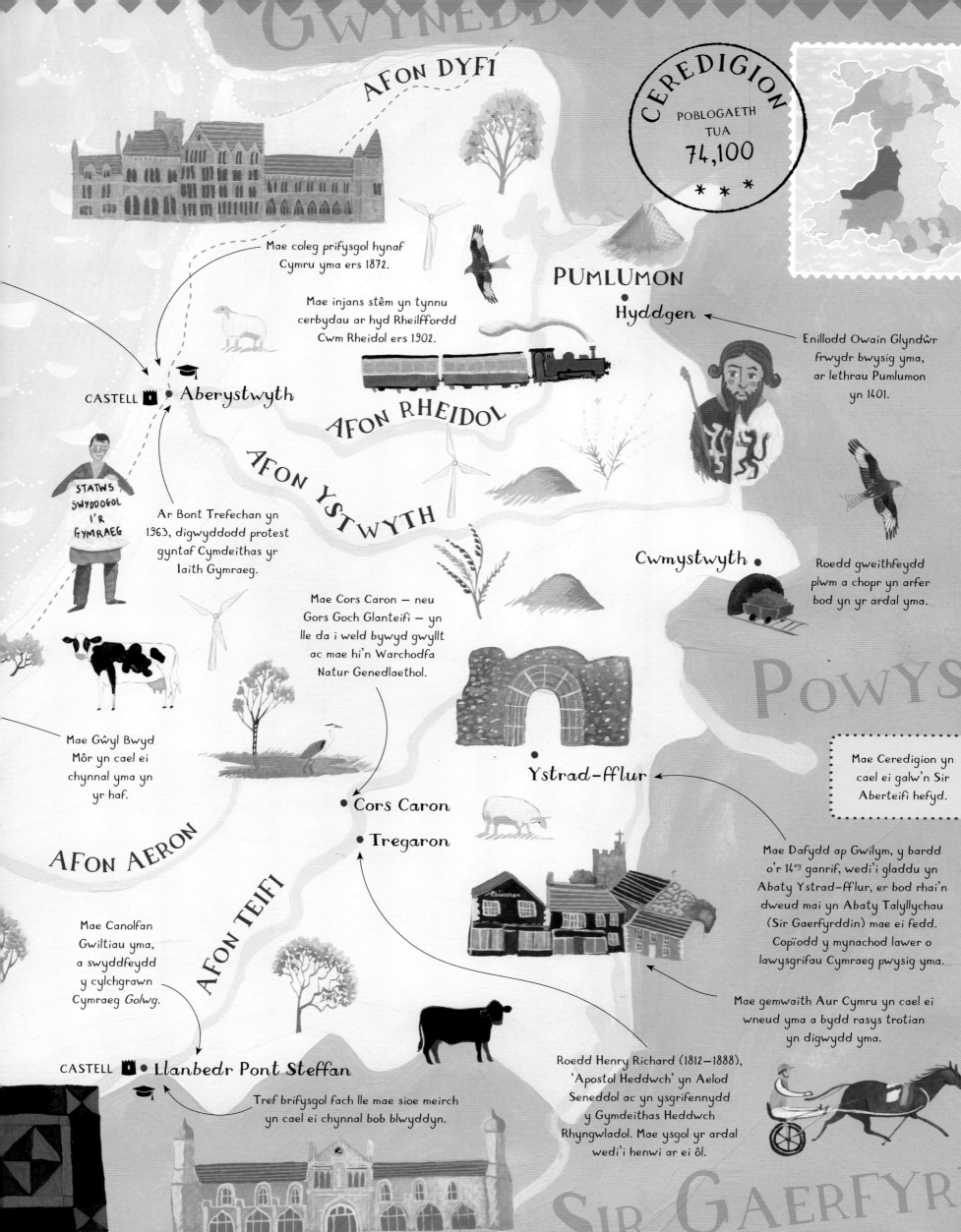

AFON DYFI

CEREDIGION

POBLOGAETH TUA

74,100

* * *

PUMLUMON

Mae coleg prifysgol hynaf Cymru yma ers 1872.

Mae injans stêm yn tynnu cerbydau ar hyd Rheilffordd Cwm Rheidol ers 1902.

Hyddgen

Enillodd Owain Glyndŵr frwydr bwysig yma, ar lethrau Pumlumon yn 1401.

CASTELL • Aberystwyth

AFON RHEIDOL

STATWS SWYDDOGOL I'R GYMRAEG

Ar Bont Trefechan yn 1963, digwyddodd protest gyntaf Cymdeithas yr Iaith Gymraeg.

AFON YSTWYTH

Cwmystwyth

Roedd gweithfeydd plwm a chopr yn arfer bod yn yr ardal yma.

Mae Cors Caron — neu Gors Goch Glanteifi — yn lle da i weld bywyd gwyllt ac mae hi'n Warchodfa Natur Genedlaethol.

Mae Gŵyl Bwyd Môr yn cael ei chynnal yma yn yr haf.

POWYS

Ystrad-fflur

Mae Ceredigion yn cael ei galw'n Sir Aberteifi hefyd.

• Cors Caron
• Tregaron

AFON AERON

Mae Canolfan Gwiltiau yma, a swyddfeydd y cylchgrawn Cymraeg *Golwg*.

AFON TEIFI

Mae Dafydd ap Gwilym, y bardd o'r 14eg ganrif, wedi'i gladdu yn Abaty Ystrad-fflur, er bod rhai'n dweud mai yn Abaty Talyllychau (Sir Gaerfyrddin) mae ei fedd. Copïodd y mynachod lawer o lawysgrifau Cymraeg pwysig yma.

Mae gemwaith Aur Cymru yn cael ei wneud yma a bydd rasys trotian yn digwydd yma.

CASTELL • Llanbedr Pont Steffan

Tref brifysgol fach lle mae sioe meirch yn cael ei chynnal bob blwyddyn.

Roedd Henry Richard (1812–1888), 'Apostol Heddwch' yn Aelod Seneddol ac yn ysgrifennydd y Gymdeithas Heddwch Rhyngwladol. Mae ysgol yr ardal wedi'i henwi ar ei ôl.

POWYS

2,000 km² (5,179 milltir²)

SIR DREFALDWYN

Cyfieithodd yr Esgob William Morgan y Beibl i'r Gymraeg yma yn 1588.

Llyn Efyrnwy ym mynyddoedd y Berwyn oedd argae dŵr cyntaf Cymru. Cafodd ei adeiladu gan Lerpwl rhwng 1881 ac 1888 er mwyn i'r ddinas gael rhagor o ddŵr.

GWYNEDD

LLYN EFYRNWY

Mae Canolfan y Dechnoleg Amgen yn dangos sut gallwn fyw heb ddinistrio'r ddaear.

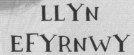

Agorodd y cynllunydd ffasiwn a'r ddynes fusnes Laura Ashley ffatri ddillad yma yn y 1960au; caeodd hi yn 2005.

• Machynlleth

Carno •

Cynhaliodd Owain Glyndŵr senedd yma yn 1404.

LLYN CLYWEDOG

SIR DREFALD

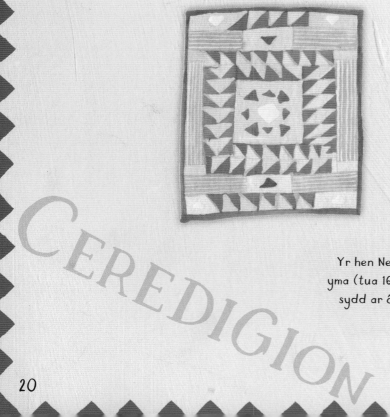

Mae llawer o gwiltiau Cymreig i'w gweld yng Nghanolfan Gelfyddydau Minerva.

Llanidloes
•

Y BERWYN

CEREDIGION

Yr hen Neuadd Farchnad yma (tua 1600) yw'r unig un sydd ar ôl yng Nghymru.

SIR

Pistyll Rhaeadr yw rhaeadr uchaf Cymru.
Mae'r dŵr yn cwympo dros 80 metr.
Mae'n un o Saith Rhyfeddod Cymru.

• Llanrhaeadr-
  ym-Mochnant

POWYS
POBLOGAETH
TUA
132,200
✱ ✱ ✱

SIR DREFALDWYN
POBLOGAETH TUA
63,800

AFON HAFREN

Gallwch ymweld â'r
castell coch canoloesol
a'r gerddi hyfryd.

CASTELL POWYS ⛫

🛩 ⛫ CASTELL
• Y Trallwng

Mae marchnadoedd anifeiliaid
yn cael eu cynnal yma.

Mae Maes Awyr
Canolbarth Cymru
gerllaw'r dref.

Cododd Llywelyn ap Gruffudd
y castell yn y 1270au.

CASTELL DOLFORWYN ⛫

CASTELL ⛫
• Trefaldwyn

Mae castell yma ers yr 11eg ganrif.

• Y Drenewydd

Roedd y diwydiant gwlân
yn bwysig iawn yn y dref
yn y 19eg ganrif.

Dechreuodd Pryce Jones y
busnes archebu drwy'r post
cyntaf yn y byd yma yn 1861.

Mae amgueddfa yma i Robert Owen,
diwydiannwr a oedd yn gofalu am ei
weithwyr ym melinau cotwm New Lanark,
yr Alban, yn y 18fed ganrif.

Mae chwe argae dŵr yn y cwm, wedi'u hadeiladu gan ddinas Birmingham ar ddiwedd y 19eg ganrif a dechrau'r 20fed ganrif.

Cwm Elan •

Abaty Cwm-hir •

LLYN CLYWEDOG

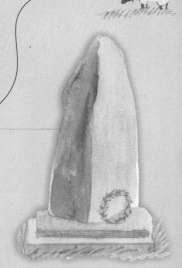

Mae Llywelyn ap Gruffudd, ein Llyw Olaf (m. 1282), wedi'i gladdu yn yr abaty.

Mae Pencampwriaethau Snorclo Cors y Byd yn digwydd ger Llanwrtyd bob gŵyl banc mis Awst.

Yma cafodd Llywelyn ap Gruffudd, ein Llyw Olaf, ei ladd yn 1282.

Cilmeri •

Llangamarch

Llanwrtyd •

Tair tref lle roedd pobl yn dod i brofi'r dyfroedd.

POWYS
2,000 km² (5,179 milltir²)
YR HEN FAESYFED A BRYCHEINIOG

Frances Hoggan o Aberhonddu oedd y fenyw gyntaf o Brydain a'r ail fenyw o Ewrop i gael gradd mewn meddygaeth.

AFON WYSG

MYNYDD EPYNT

Mae Gŵyl Jazz Aberhonddu yn boblogaidd iawn bob mis Awst.

PARC CENEDLAETHOL BANNAU BRYCHEINIOG

Daeth Tommy a Jeff Morgan o hyd i'r ogofâu hyn yn 1912.

Mae eglwys gadeiriol yma.

Roedd pobl yn arfer gweithio yn y pyllau glo a'r ffatri gwneud clo</br>ciau yn yr ardal hon.

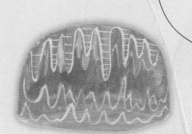

Ogofâu Dan yr Ogof •

Ystradgynlais •

Llandrindod yw prif dref Powys. Yn oes Victoria roedd y dref yn enwog am ei dyfroedd iachus.

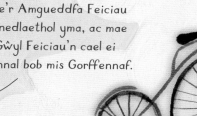

Mae'r Amgueddfa Feiciau Genedlaethol yma, ac mae Gŵyl Feiciau'n cael ei chynnal bob mis Gorffennaf.

• Llandrindod

Mae Sioe Frenhinol Cymru yn cael ei chynnal yma bob mis Gorffennaf ers 1963.

POWYS
POBLOGAETH TUA
132,200
✴ ✴ ✴

• Llanelwedd
• Llanfair-ym-Muallt

SIR FAESYFED
POBLOGAETH TUA
24,900

AFON GWY

BRYCHEINIOG
POBLOGAETH TUA
43,500

L L O E G R

🏰 CASTELL BRONLLYS

Castell mwnt a beili o'r 12fed ganrif.

Llyn Syfaddan yw'r llyn naturiol mwyaf yn ne Cymru.

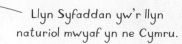

• Aberhonddu

LLYN SYFADDAN

🏰 CASTELL TRETŴR

Pen-y-Fan

CRONFA DDŴR TAL-Y-BONT

🏰 CASTELL
Crucywel

Cafodd Syr George Everest (1790–1866) ei eni yma. Buodd e'n gweithio fel tirfesurydd yn India. Cafodd mynydd uchaf y byd ei enwi ar ei ôl yn 1865. Chomolungma yw enw'r mynydd yn iaith Tibet.

Mynydd uchaf de Cymru — mae'n 886m o uchder.

BLAENAU

SIR FYNWY

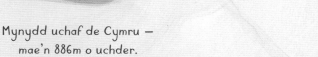

Gallwch hwylio o'r porthladd yma i Rosslare, yn Iwerddon.

Glaniodd milwyr Ffrainc yma yn 1797, y tro diwethaf i filwyr tramor droedio tir Prydain. Cafodd rhai milwyr eu dal gan fenywod lleol, o dan arweiniad Jemeima Nicholas. Cafodd y Ffrancwyr eu trechu'n hawdd.

Pen Strwmbl

Abergwaun •

• **Tregwynt**

Cwm Gwaun •

Mae melin wlân enwog yma, a'r cynnyrch yn cael ei werthu ledled y byd.

Roedd calch yn cael ei losgi yn yr hen odynau pan oedd Solfach yn harbwr prysur.

CRONFA DDŴR LLYS-Y-FRÂN

Tyddewi •

Solfach

Dinas leiaf Prydain. Yma mae cadeirlan Dewi Sant, nawddsant Cymru. Roedd Dewi'n byw yma yn y 6ed ganrif.

Ynys Dewi

BAE SAIN FFRAID

Prif dref Sir Benfro. Mae castell yma ers 1110.

CLEDDAU

Mae palod ac adar drycin Manaw'n nythu yma. Gallwch fynd draw ar gwch i'w gweld.

Ynys Sgomer

Hwlffordd •
CASTELL 🏰

IVEN

Mae purfa olew yma. Mae dwy afon Cleddau'n llifo i'r hafan — Cleddau Ddu a Cleddau Wen.

Glaniodd Harri Tudur yma yn 1485. Teithiodd i Bosworth, ennill brwydr a'i goroni'n Frenin Harri'r Seithfed. Beth am ddysgu hwylio yma?

• **Dale**

Aberdaugleddau

Ynys Sgogwm

Doc Penfro
• 🏰 CASTELL PENFRO

🏰 CASTELL CAERIW

Mae llongau'n hwylio oddi yma i Rosslare yn Iwerddon.

Eglwys fechan yn y graig. Roedd Sant Gofan yn byw mewn ogof gerllaw yn y 6ed ganrif.

Eglwys Sant Gofan

24

CEREDIGION

Mae abaty yma ers 1115.
Roedd y mynachod yn
berchen ar Ynys Bŷr.

● Llandudoch

AFON TEIFI

SIR BENFRO
POBLOGAETH
TUA
124,000
* * *

CASTELL
CILGERRAN 🏰

LLWYBR ARFORDIR SIR BENFRO

● Pentre Ifan

Pentref bach sy'n brif
ganolfan y Preseli.

Cromlech o'r Oes Neolithig.
Mae'n cynnwys 7 carreg ac
mae tua 5,500 mlwydd oed.

MYNYDDOEDD
PRESELI

● Crymych

Mae Llwybr Arfordir
Sir Benfro yn 186
milltir o hyd.

Mae olion o'r Oes Haearn
a'r Oes Efydd i'w gweld
yma. Mae cerrig o'r
Preseli yng Nghôr y
Cewri (Stonehenge).

Ers 1952, mae Parc
Cenedlaethol Arfordir Penfro
yn gwarchod yr ardal.

Mae pobl Cwm
Gwaun yn dathlu'r
Hen Galan ar
13 Ionawr.

SIR GAERFYRDDIN

CLEDDAU DDU

🏰 CASTELL
LLAWHADEN

Mae tatws cynnar yn cael eu
tyfu yn Sir Benfro oherwydd
bod yr hinsawdd yn fwyn yma.

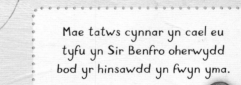

● Arberth

Tref siopa brysur. Mae rhai arbenigwyr
yn dweud mai yma roedd prif lys
Pwyll, Pendefig Dyfed.

Tref glan môr gaerog
(mae wal o'i chwmpas).

↓

SIR BENFRO

1,590 km² (610 milltir²)

● Dinbych-y-pysgod

🏰 CASTELL
MAENORBŶR

● Ynys Bŷr

Mae mynachod yn byw yma. Maen nhw'n gwneud
persawr a siocled i'w gwerthu i dwristiaid.

SIR BENFRO

Mae rhaeadr hyfryd ar afon Teifi yma. Mae'r cwrwgl yn cael ei ddefnyddio fan hyn fel cwch pysgota.

Mae Amgueddfa Wlân Cymru yn hen felin wlân Cambria. Mae'n adrodd hanes y diwydiant gwlân yn y rhan hon o Ddyffryn Teifi.

Cenarth •

CASTELL 🏰

Castellnewydd Emlyn

• Dre-fach Felindre

Llanllwni •

Yn 1839, ymosododd protestwyr ar dollborth yr Efail-wen dair gwaith oherwydd bod rhaid talu am deithio ar ffyrdd tyrpeg. Dyma ddechrau Terfysgoedd Rebeca. Roedd pawb yn gwisgo dillad menywod rhag i neb eu hadnabod.

Mae cofeb y tu allan i'r Neuadd Sirol i gofio 1966, pan ddaeth Gwynfor Evans yn aelod seneddol cyntaf Plaid Cymru.

Mae pysgotwyr yn defnyddio cwrwgl fel cwch ar afon Tywi.

Tref hynaf Cymru. Yn yr hen briordy, ysgrifennodd mynach Lyfr Du Caerfyrddin, llawysgrif Gymraeg hynaf Cymru.

• Yr Efail-wen

Tua OC 940, casglodd y brenin Hywel Dda bobl o bob rhan o Gymru yma i roi trefn ar gyfraith y Cymry. Mae canolfan a gardd Hywel Dda yma heddiw.

Roedd y dewin Myrddin yn dod o Gaerfyrddin ac mae hanes yr hen dderwen yn gysylltiedig ag ef.

🎓 • Caerfyrddin

CASTELL

Hendy-gwyn ar Daf

AFON TAF

Mae hanes o gasglu cocos yma. Roedd fferi'n arfer croesi afon Tywi i Lansteffan.

Gardd Fotaneg Genedlaethol Cymru •

Yn 1927, cafodd y gyrrwr rasio John Parry Thomas ei ladd wrth geisio torri record cyflymdra'r byd ar y traeth yn ei gar, Babs.

Llanddowror •

Llangyndeyrn •

Y Tymbl •

CASTELL 🏰 Talacharn

Llansteffan

CASTELL 🏰 •

Glanyfferi

GWENDRAETH FACH

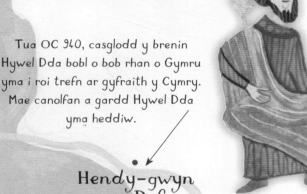

Pentywyn

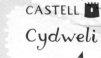

DIM BODDI'R CWM!

BAE CAERFYRDDIN

CASTELL 🏰 Cydweli

GWENDRAETH FAWR

Yn 1137, lladdwyd y Dywysoges Gwenllïan wrth arwain byddin ei gŵr, Gruffudd ap Rhys, yn erbyn y Normaniaid.

Porth Tywyn •

Llanelli •

Yn 1928, glaniodd Amelia Earhart yma ar ôl hedfan ar draws yr Iwerydd. Hi oedd y fenyw gyntaf i wneud hynny.

Agorodd Ysgol Gynradd Gymraeg Llanelli (Ysgol Dewi Sant wedyn) yn 1947. Hi oedd yr ysgol gynradd Gymraeg gyntaf i'w hagor gan gyngor sir.

Roedd Twm Siôn Cati (1530–1610) yn arfer cuddio mewn ogof yma ar ôl dwyn arian y bobl gyfoethog i'w roi i'r bobl dlawd.

LLYn BRIAnNE

SIR GAERFYRDDIN
POBLOGAETH TUA
185,600
★ ★ ★

Roedd y Rhufeiniaid yn arfer cloddio am aur yma.

• Ystrad-ffin

Mwynfeydd
Aur Dolau Cothi

POWYS

Gallwch weld adfeilion abaty o 1180 yma.

AFON COTHI

AFON TYWI

AFON HIRAF CYMRU (68 MILLTIR)

Talyllychau

• Llanymddyfri

CASTELL

Roedd porthmyn yn arfer galw yn Llanymddyfri ar eu ffordd i Lundain i werthu'r anifeiliaid roedden nhw'n eu gyrru.

Mae William Williams, Pantycelyn, yr emynydd enwog, yn dod o'r ardal hon.

Llyn y Fan Fach
Myddfai

• Llandeilo
CASTELL DINEFWR

Gallwch ymweld â Chastell Dinefwr, prif lys tywysogion y Deheubarth yn yr Oesoedd Canol, a gweld y gwartheg gwynion prin sydd yma.

Yn ôl y chwedl, daeth menyw o'r llyn i briodi bugail o'r enw Rhiwallon. Cawson nhw feibion a ddaeth yn feddygon enwog yn ardal Myddfai.

Dechreuodd rygbi gael ei chwarae am y tro cyntaf yng Nghymru yng Ngholeg Llanymddyfri tua 1850.

CASTELL DRYSLWYN

CASTELL
CARREG CENNEN

Mae Tŷ Gwydr anferth yma a Phlas Pilipala.

Prif dref Dyffryn Aman, lle roedd y diwydiant glo'n arfer bod yn bwysig.

Rhydaman

Mae'r cerflun enfawr o lamp glöwr ger mynedfa Parc Coetir Mynydd Mawr yn dangos bod y diwydiant glo'n arfer bod yn bwysig yng Nghwm Gwendraeth.

CASTELL-NEDD

Rhwng 1959 ac 1964, brwydrodd y bobl leol yn erbyn boddi'r ardal i greu cronfa ddŵr, a llwyddo!

🛆 M4

M4

SIR GAERFYRDDIN

2,395 km² (925 milltir²)

Roedd Llanelli'n enwog am gynhyrchu tunplat, ac roedd y dref yn cael ei galw'n 'Tinopolis'. Heddiw, mae'n gartref i dîm rygbi rhanbarthol y Scarlets.

Mae Sir Gaerfyrddin yn cael ei galw'n 'Sir Gâr' hefyd.

ABER

DINAS A SIR ABERTAWE

380 km² (150 milltir²)

Yn 1947, aeth 8 dyn o fad achub y Mwmbwls allan mewn storm i geisio achub criw o 39 dyn ar long *SS Samtampa* ger Porth-cawl. Collodd pob un o ddynion y bad achub a'r llong eu bywydau. Mae ffenestri gwydr lliw yn coffáu hyn yn eglwys Ystumllwynarth.

SIR GAER...

🎓 **Prifysgol Abertawe**

Mae Adran Beirianneg Prifysgol Abertawe wedi bod yn helpu i ddatblygu Bloodhound SSC. Car yw hwn sy'n mynd i geisio teithio 1,000 milltir yr awr, a thorri record cyflymder ar y tir.

Cafodd canol Abertawe ei ddinistrio ym mis Chwefror 1941, yn ystod yr Ail Ryfel Byd.

Dylan Thomas

Cafodd Dylan Thomas (1914–53), y bardd a'r awdur Saesneg, ei eni a'i fagu yn Abertawe.

Swansea Jack

Ci oedd Swansea Jack a achubodd fachgen 12 oed a oedd wedi cwympo i'r dociau yn y 1930au, a rhagor o bobl eto, efallai. Mae cofeb iddo ar y prom. Nawr, Swansea Jacks yw'r enw ar bobl Abertawe.

🏰 CASTELL WEBLE

• **Llangynydd**

Lle gwych i fynd i syrffio!

BAE RHOSILI

PENRHYN GŴYR

Mae Penrhyn Gŵyr yn Ardal o Harddwch Naturiol Eithriadol.

Un o draethau harddaf Gŵyr.

CASTELL PENNARD 🏰

Pen Pyrod   **Rhosili**

CEFN BRYN

Bae'r Tri Chlogwyn •

Daeth sgerbwd 'Dynes Goch Paviland' i'r golwg yn 1823. Mewn gwirionedd dyn ifanc oedd y sgerbwd. Roedd yn byw tua 24,000 CC.

• **Ogof Twll yr Afr, Pen-y-fai**

• **Port Einon**

BAE OXWICH

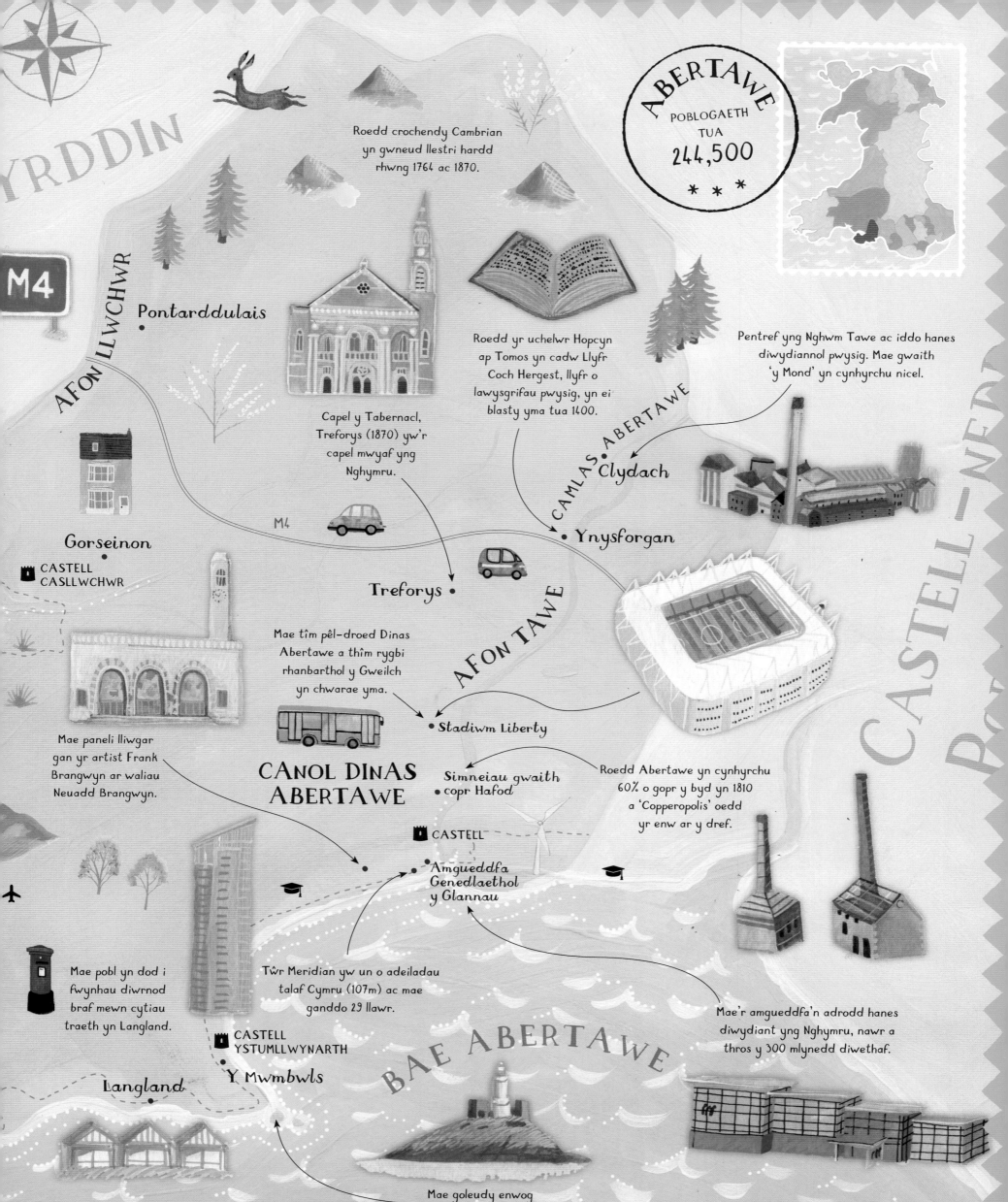

ABERTAWE
POBLOGAETH
TUA
244,500
★★★

Roedd crochendy Cambrian yn gwneud llestri hardd rhwng 1764 ac 1870.

Roedd yr uchelwr Hopcyn ap Tomos yn cadw Llyfr Coch Hergest, llyfr o lawysgrifau pwysig, yn ei blasty yma tua 1400.

Pentref yng Nghwm Tawe ac iddo hanes diwydiannol pwysig. Mae gwaith 'y Mond' yn cynhyrchu nicel.

PYRDDIN

AFON LLWCHWR

M4

Pontarddulais

Capel y Tabernacl, Treforys (1870) yw'r capel mwyaf yng Nghymru.

CAMLAS ABERTAWE

Clydach

Ynysforgan

Gorseinon

CASTELL CASLLWCHWR

M4

Treforys

Mae tîm pêl-droed Dinas Abertawe a thîm rygbi rhanbarthol y Gweilch yn chwarae yma.

AFON TAWE

CASTELL-NEDD

Mae paneli lliwgar gan yr artist Frank Brangwyn ar waliau Neuadd Brangwyn.

CANOL DINAS ABERTAWE

Stadiwm Liberty

Simneiau gwaith copr Hafod

Roedd Abertawe yn cynhyrchu 60% o gopr y byd yn 1810 a 'Copperopolis' oedd yr enw ar y dref.

CASTELL

Amgueddfa Genedlaethol y Glannau

Mae pobl yn dod i fwynhau diwrnod braf mewn cytiau traeth yn Langland.

Twr Meridian yw un o adeiladau talaf Cymru (107m) ac mae ganddo 29 llawr.

Mae'r amgueddfa'n adrodd hanes diwydiant yng Nghymru, nawr a thros y 300 mlynedd diwethaf.

CASTELL YSTUMLLWYNARTH

BAE ABERTAWE

Langland

Y Mwmbwls

Mae goleudy enwog ar Ben y Mwmbwls.

29

CASTELL–NEDD PORT TALBOT

442 km² (171 milltir²)

CASTELL-NEDD PORT TALBOT ★
POBLOGAETH TUA 141,600 ★ ★ ★

SIR GAERFYRDDIN

POWYS

CWM NEDD

ABERTAW

CAMLAS ABERTAWE

AFON TAWE

Pontneddfechan

Blaen-gwrach

Resolfen

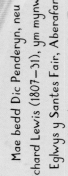

Onllwyn

Mae bedd Dic Penderyn, neu Richard Lewis (1807–31), ym mynwent Eglwys y Santes Fair, Aberafan. Pan oedd yn löwr ym Merthyr Tudful, cymerodd ran mewn terfysg yno a chafodd ei gyhuddo o niweidio milwr. Cafodd ei grogi am hyn yng Nghaerdydd, er ei fod yn ddieuog. Ei eiriau olaf oedd "O Arglwydd, dyma gamwedd!"

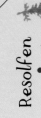

Mae Cwm Nedd yn enwog am ei sgydau (rhaeadrau) hardd. Gallwch gerdded y tu ôl i Sgwd yr Eira.

Yn Amgueddfa Glofa Cefn Coed cewch wybod am hanes pwll glo caled dyfnaf y byd ar un adeg.

Y Creunant

Ystalyfera

Cwmllynfell

Gwauncaegurwen

Cafodd y chwaraewr rygbi Gareth Edwards ei eni yma.

Roedd gweithfeydd dur a thunplat yma o 1860 tan 1962.

Pontardawe

Gallwch ddod yma i weld y rhaeadr a'r hen waith tun.

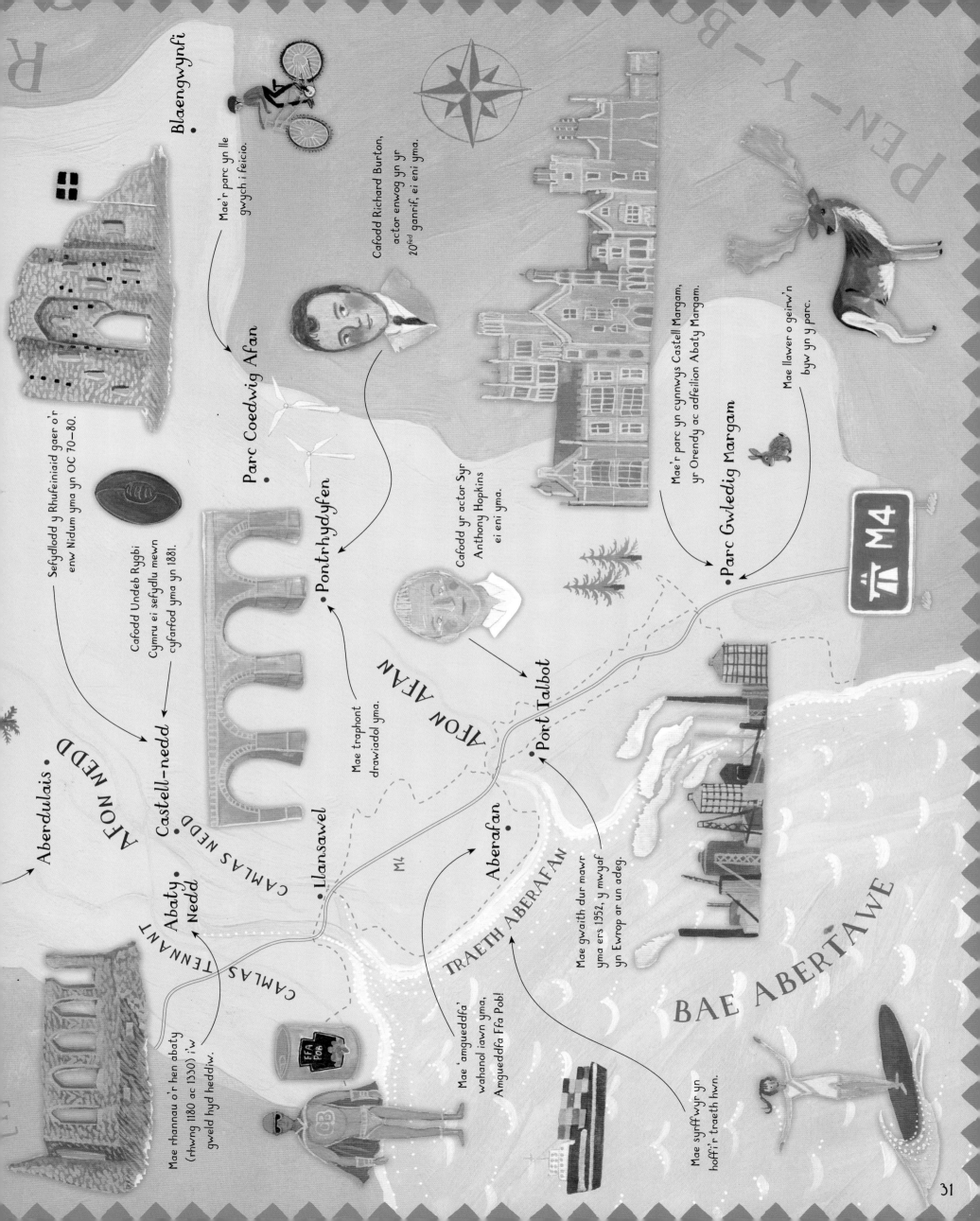

Blaengwynfi •

Mae'r parc yn lle gwych i feicio.

Cafodd Richard Burton, actor enwog yn yr 20^{fed} ganrif, ei eni yma.

Mae llawer o geirw'n byw yn y parc.

Mae'r parc yn cynnwys Castell Margam, yr Orendy ac adfeilion Abaty Margam.

Parc Coedwig Afan

Parc Gwledig Margam

Sefydlodd y Rhufeiniaid gaer o'r enw Nidum yma yn OC 70–80.

Cafodd Undeb Rugbi Cymru ei sefydlu mewn cyfarfod yma yn 1881.

• Pontrhydyfen

Cafodd yr actor Syr Anthony Hopkins ei eni yma.

AFON NEDD

Aberdulais •

Castell-nedd •

Mae traphont drawiadol yma.

AFON AFAN

• Port Talbot

CAMLAS NEDD

Abaty • Nedd

• Llansawel

M4

Mae rhannau o'r hen abaty (rhwng 1180 ac 1330) i'w gweld hyd heddiw.

CAMLAS TENNANT

Mae 'amgueddfa' wahanol iawn yma, Amgueddfa Ffa Pobl!

Aberafan •

Mae gwaith dur mawr yma ers 1952, y mwyaf yn Ewrop ar un adeg.

TRAETH ABERAFAN

BAE ABERTAWE

Mae syrff-wyr yn hoff'i'r traeth hwn.

Pen-y-Bont ar Ogwr

246 km² (95 milltir²)

• Caerau

Roedd haearn, tunplat a glo yn cael eu cynhyrchu yma ar un adeg.

Maesteg •

Cadwodd yr ardal hon draddodiad y Fari Lwyd adeg y Nadolig a'r flwyddyn newydd.

Llangynwyd

CASTELL

ABERTAWE

BAE

GWELL-NEDD

PORT TALBOT

Mae llwybr arbennig yma gyda cherfluniau pren sy'n dathlu hanes y warchodfa. Roedd pwll glo yma ar un adeg, ond nawr mae'n ardal bwysig i fywyd gwyllt.

Gwarchodfa Natur Parc Slip

Roedd hen dref gaerog gerllaw, ond cafodd ei chladdu dan dwyni tywod ar ôl stormydd ddiwedd y 14^{eg} ganrif.

TWYNI CYNFFIG

• Mynydd Cynffig

M4

Cafodd y Pafiliwn ei godi yn y 1930au.

Porthladd i allforio glo a haearn oedd yma'n wreiddiol. Daeth yn dref glan môr boblogaidd yn yr 20^{fed} ganrif. Roedd llawer o weithwyr cymoedd de Cymru a'u teuluoedd yn dod yma.

Ym Mhlasty'r Sger yn y 18^{fed} ganrif roedd Elisabeth Williams, 'Y Ferch o'r Sger' yn byw. Roedd hi eisiau priodi'r saer a'r telynor tlawd, Thomas Evans, ond gorfododd ei rhieni hi i briodi dyn cefnog o Gastell-nedd.

MÔR HAFREN

Porth-cawl

Merthyr Mawr •

Mae maes carafannau Bae Trecco yn un o'r rhai mwyaf yn Ewrop.

BAE TRECCO

RHONDDA CYNON TAF

Nant-y-moel

Pontycymer

Enillodd Lynn Davies o Nant-y-moel fedal aur am y naid hir yn y Gemau Olympaidd yn Tokyo yn 1964. Fe oedd yr athletwr unigol cyntaf o Gymru i ennill medal aur Olympaidd.

149

Mae llawer o ffatrïoedd a busnesau yn yr ardal gan ei bod yn agos at draffordd yr M4.

• Llangeinwyr

Canolfan fawr gerllaw'r M4 yw McArthurGlen gyda siopau, sinema a bwytai.

• Glynogwr

Yn ystod Gwrthryfel Glyndŵr, buodd y castell o dan warchae ddwywaith rhwng 1404 ac 1405.

DAVIES

AFON OGWR

M4

• Sarn

CASTELL
• Coety

CASTELL NEWYDD
• Pen-y-bont

Mae Aled Siôn Davies yn athletwr Paralympaidd. Mae wedi bod yn Bencampwr Byd mewn mabolgampau taflu ac enillodd sawl medal aur mewn Gemau Paralympaidd.

Cododd y brenin Harri II Gastellnewydd ar Ogwr yma yn y 1180au.

• Gwersyll Island Farm

Pentref hardd gyda llawer o dai a bythynnod to gwellt. Mae twyni tywod gerllaw.

Roedd carcharorion o'r Almaen yma yn ystod yr Ail Ryfel Byd. Adeiladodd y carcharorion dwnnel ac ym mis Mawrth 1945 llwyddodd mwy i ddianc oddi yma nag o unrhyw garchar arall. Cawson nhw i gyd eu dal.

PEN-Y-BONT AR OGWR
POBLOGAETH TUA 74,100
★ ★ ★

BRO MORGANNWG

33

Bro MorGannwG

335 km² (129 milltir²)

RHONDDA C

AFON OGWR

-Y-BONT

R OGWR

Mae Ewenni'n enwog ers canrifoedd am wneud crochenwaith. Mae dau grochendy yma o hyd.

Ewenni

Bwrdeistref bwysig ers yr Oesoedd Canol. Mae rhan o hen furiau'r dref i'w gweld o hyd. Mae'n dref siopa boblogaidd heddiw.

CASTELL
Aberogwr

Cafodd Priordy Ewenni ei sefydlu yn y 12^{fed} ganrif. Mae darlun gan J. M. W. Turner, yr arlunydd enwog, yn dangos y priordy ar ddiwedd y 18^{fed} ganrif.

Y Bont-faen

CASTELL
LLANFLEIDDAN

Llandŵ

Ar Fryn Owain, cynhaliodd Iolo Morganwg yr Orsedd gyntaf yng Nghymru yn 1795.

Mae ffosiliau i'w gweld ar y traeth yma.

Y Wig

Gallwch yrru cert o gwmpas Cylchffordd Rasio Llandŵ.

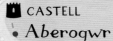

LLWYBR ARFORDIR CYMRU

Roedd gan Illtud, y sant, ganolfan bwysig iawn yma o ddiwedd y 5^{ed} ganrif.

Llanilltud Fawr

Mae gan Aston Martin ffatri i adeiladu ceir yma.

Sain Tathan

Yn yr haf, gallwch fynd ar daith ar long bleser o bier Penarth.

MÔR HAFREN

34

BRO MORGANNWG
POBLOGAETH
TUA
128,500
★ ★ ★

🛣 M4

AFON ELÁI

Mae'r safle dros 6,000 o flynyddoedd oed. Mae'r maen capan yn un o'r trymaf ym Mhrydain.

Lle mae'r marina nawr, roedd dociau rhwng canol y 19[eg] ganrif a chanol yr 20[fed] ganrif.

Llanbedr-y-fro

Drope

Mae pier ym Mhenarth ers 1898, pan oedd hi'n dref wyliau boblogaidd. Heddiw, mae sinema, oriel a chaffi yma.

Gallwch ymweld â'r gerddi hardd, yr ardd goed a'r plasty o oes Victoria yma.

Siambr Gladdu Tinkinswood

Gerddi Dyffryn

Penarth •

Roedd y dociau'n bwysig i allforio glo ac i fewnforio bananas yn yr 20[fed] ganrif.

Llynnoedd, Parc Gwledig a Phentref Canoloesol Cosmeston •

Maes Awyr Cymru Caerdydd yw prif faes awyr Cymru.

Byddwch yn ofalus! Gallwch groesi draw i'r ynys, ond dim ond pan fydd y môr ar drai.

Larnog •

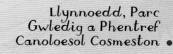

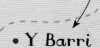

Y Barri •

Ynys Sili •

Y Rhws •

• Ynys y Barri

Kathleen Thomas oedd y person cyntaf i nofio ar draws Môr Hafren, o Benarth i Weston-super-Mare, yn 1927, mewn 7 awr ac 20 munud.

Mae pobl yn mwynhau diwrnod ar lan y môr yn Ynys y Barri.

Ynys Echni (CAERDYDD)

Yn 1897, anfonodd Guglielmo Marconi y neges radio gyntaf yn y byd ar draws y dŵr o Drwyn Larnog ger Penarth i'r ynys hon.

RHONDDA CYNON TAF

POBLOGAETH TUA 238,300

MERTHYR TUDFUL

POWYS

CAERFFILI

AFON TAF

Gweithiodd Elizabeth Andrews (1882–1960) o Hirwaun yn galed i wneud bywyd yn haws i fenywod. Llwyddodd i gael baddonau mewn pyllau glo, a'r ysgol feithrin gyntaf yn y Rhondda.

Mae Rasys Nos Galan yn cael eu cynnal yma, i gofio'r rhedwr Guto Nyth Brân, Griffith Morgan. Bu farw'n 37 oed yn 1737 ar ôl rhedeg yn gyflymach na dyn ar gefn ceffyl.

• Aberpennar

Tref ddiwydiannol bwysig yn y 18fed a'r 19eg ganrif.

Mae Parc Gwledig Cwm Dâr yn lle gwych i gerdded, beicio a gwylio hebogau.

• Aberdâr

PARC CENEDLAETHOL BANNAU BRYCHEINIOG

Penderyn •

AFON CYNON

Pen-y-waun •

Gallwch feicio neu gerdded ar hyd Llwybr Cynon sy'n 9 milltir o hyd rhwng Abercynon a Hirwaun.

Hirwaun •

AFON RHONDDA FACH

RHONDDA CYNON TAF

424 km² (164 milltir²)

Treherbert •

Caeodd Glofa'r Twr, pwll glo dwfn olaf Prydain, yn 2008.

POWYS

MERTHYR TUDFUL

NEDD PORT TALBOT

Nantgarw

Yn Amgueddfa Crochendy Nantgarw gallwch weld y porslen gwych a oedd yn cael ei gynhyrchu yma rhwng 1813 ac 1820.

Mae cofeb ym Mharc Ynysangharad i Evan James a James James. Cyfansoddodd y tad a'r mab yr anthem genedlaethol, 'Hen Wlad fy Nhadau', yn 1856.

Agorodd Ysgol Rhydfelen, yr ysgol gyfun Gymraeg gyntaf yn ne Cymru, ger Pontypridd yn 1962. Newidiodd ei henw i Ysgol Garth Olwg pan symudodd i Bentre'r Eglwys yn 2006.

Abercynon

Mae Syr Tom Jones, y canwr byd-enwog, yn dod o Bontypridd.

Lido Ponty, a'i dri phwll nofio awyr agored, yw Lido Cenedlaethol Cymru.

Pontypridd

Llanilltud Faerdref

Mae'r dref yn enwog am hen bont (1756) William Edwards gyda'i bwa sengl 42.3m o hyd.

AFON RHONDDA

Ferndale

Lladdwyd 178 o lowyr mewn ffrwydrad yn y pwll glo yma yn 1867, a lladdwyd 53 hefyd yn 1869.

Trehafod

Porth

CASTELL

Llantrisant

Pont-y-clun

Treorci

Tonypandy

Tonyrefail

AFON ELÁI

Llanharan

Symudodd llawer o bobl i'r ardal i weithio yn y gweithfeydd haearn a'r pyllau glo yn y 19eg a'r 20fed ganrif.

Yn ystod terfysgoedd yma yn 1910, aeth glowyr oedd yn streicio i gael mwy o gyflog ar hyd y brif stryd, a difrodi 60 o siopau.

Beth am fynd o dan ddaear yn hen bwll glo Lewis Merthyr ym Mharc Treftadaeth Cwm Rhondda?

Gallwch ymweld â'r Bathdy Brenhinol sy'n cynhyrchu pob darn arian ar gyfer y Deyrnas Unedig a llawer o wledydd eraill.

M4

POWYS

MERTHYR TUDFUL
POBLOGAETH TUA 59,800 ★ ★ ★ ★

Merthyr Tudful yw'r sir sydd â'r boblogaeth leiaf yng Nghymru. Ond yn 1851, pan oedd Merthyr yn brifddinas cynhyrchu haearn, hi oedd y dref fwyaf poblog Cymru.

Yn 1840au, gwaith haearn Cwmni Haearn Dowlais oedd y mwyaf yn y byd gyda 5,000 o weithwyr.

Gwraig rheolwr gwaith haearn Dowlais oedd y Foneddiges Charlotte Guest (1812–95). Cyfieithodd hi chwedlau'r Mabinogi o'r Gymraeg i'r Saesneg.

Cafodd cadwyni Pont Menai (Ynys Môn) eu gwneud yng ngwaith haearn Penydarren.

Mae'r cynllunydd ffasiwn Julien Macdonald yn dod o Ferthyr yn wreiddiol.

Cafodd Castell Morlais ei godi yn y 1280au gan Gilbert de Clare.

CRONFA DDŵR PONTSTICILL

• Pontsticill

Mae prif orsaf Rheilffordd Bannau Brycheiniog yma.

BRECON MOUNTAIN RAILWAY

CASTELL MORLAIS
• Pant

• Dowlais

Roedd caer Rufeinig yma tua OC 75.

Penydarren

• Merthyr Tudful

PARC CENEDLAETHOL BANNAU BRYCHEINIOG

Cefncoedycymer •

Y Parc •

TAF FECHAN

CRONFA DDŵR LLWYN-ONN

Gallwch ymweld â'r bwthyn lle ganwyd Joseph Parry (1841–1903), cyfansoddwr y gân 'Myfanwy'.

TAF FAWR

Mae cwrs rhaffau isel yma.

Canolfan Ymwelwyr Garwnant •

Amgueddfa ac oriel gelf yw Castell Cyfarthfa heddiw. Yn wreiddiol roedd y plasty enfawr yn gartref i deulu Crawshay, meistri haearn Merthyr.

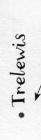

Mae canolfan ddringo yn hen lofa Trelewis, gyda waliau 18 metr o uchder.

Yn 1804, gwnaeth Richard Trevithick yr arbrawf cyntaf yn y byd gyda locomotif ager yma. Teithiodd yr injan yn 8km yr awr, dros 14km o Ferthyr i Navigation ar Gamlas Sir Forgannwg. Tynnodd 10 tunnell fetrig o haearn a thua 70 o deithwyr hefyd.

Digwyddodd trychineb ofnadwy yma ar 21 Hydref 1966. Llithrodd gwastraff glo o dip glofa Merthyr a dinistrio ffem, tai, ysgol gynradd Pant-glas a rhan o'r ysgol uwchradd. Cafodd 116 o blant a 28 oedolyn eu lladd.

• Bedlinog

• Trelewis

• Treharris

Daeth Keir Hardie yn aelod seneddol sosialaidd cyntaf Cymru yn 1900. Roedd yn dod o'r Alban yn wreiddiol.

AFON TAF

Aber-fan •

Roedd gan gwmni Hoover ffatri fawr ym Merthyr rhwng 1948 a 2009.

Mae canolfan feicio mynydd yn yr ardal.

Mae Merthyr yn enwog am gynhyrchu tecstilau.

Cafodd Laura Ashley, y cynllunydd ffasiwn, ei geni ym Merthyr.

MERTHYR TUDFUL

111 km² (43 milltir²)

Mae'n debyg mai santes oedd Tudful, merch i'r brenin Brychan o'r 5ed ganrif.

Mae cerflun yn y dref i gofio Johnny Owen, pencampwr bocsio pwysau bantam Cymru, Prydain, y Gymanwlad ac Ewrop. Bu farw ar ôl mynd i goma wrth ymladd am bencampwriaeth y byd yn Los Angeles yn 1980.

Bocsiwr enwog arall o'r sir yw Howard Winstone. Eddie Thomas o Ferthyr oedd hyfforddwr y ddau.

RHONDDA CYNON TAF

Llwybr beicio poblogaidd, 55 milltir o hyd, o Fae Caerdydd i Aberhonddu.

Cafodd Castell Coch, fel mae e heddiw, ei godi yn niwedd y 19^{eg} ganrif i gynllun gan William Burges, ond mae castell yma ers y 12^{fed} ganrif.

CASTELL COCH

Tongwynlais

Pentyrch

Prifddinas Cymru ers 1955. Mae traean poblogaeth Cymru yn byw yn ardal ddinesig Caerdydd.

Mae cartref tîm criced Morgannwg yng Ngerddi Soffia.

Radur

M4

AFON TAF

Yn y gadeirlan, mae bwa concrid sy'n dal *Majestas*, cerflun gan Jacob Epstein.

Cafodd castell Tuduraidd ei godi yma yn y 1580au. Mae Amgueddfa Werin Cymru yma ers 1947.

Llandaf

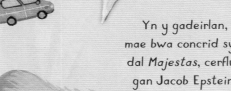

Sain Ffagan

AFON ELÁI

Gerddi Soffia

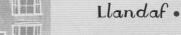

Parc yr Arfau

BRO MORGANNWG

Stadiwm Chwaraeon Rhyngwladol Caerdydd

Stadiwm Dinas Caerdydd

Cartref tîm pêl-droed Dinas Caerdydd.

Parc yr Arfau yw cartref tîm rygbi rhanbarthol Gleision Caerdydd. Roedd tîm rygbi Cymru'n arfer chwarae yma cyn codi Stadiwm Principality.

Mae Gareth Bale, y pêl-droediwr byd-enwog, yn dod o Gaerdydd.

Mae lle i 74,500 o bobl yn y stadiwm a agorodd yn 1999. Stadiwm y Mileniwm oedd yr enw'n wreiddiol.

DINAS A SIR
CAERDYDD

140 km² (54 milltir²)

Shree Swaminarayan Mandir yw'r deml Hindŵaidd gyntaf yng Nghymru, a'r fwyaf hefyd.

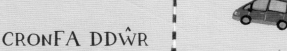

Docian Caerdydd oedd ym Mae Caerdydd yn wreiddiol. Cyn y Rhyfel Byd Cyntaf, yn 1913, cafodd dros 10 miliwn o dunelli metrig o lo o gymoedd de Cymru eu hallforio.

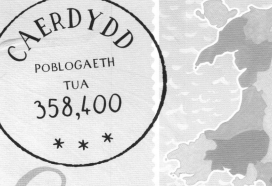

CAERDYDD
POBLOGAETH TUA
358,400
★ ★ ★

CRONFA DDŴR LLANISIEN

• Llys-faen

M4

• Pontprennau

Llanisien

• Llaneirwg

Cafodd yr adeiladau dinesig eu codi yn nechrau'r 20^{fed} ganrif.

Yn Amgueddfa Genedlaethol Caerdydd mae casgliadau cenedlaethol Cymru ym meysydd celf, daeareg a bywyd gwyllt.

LLYN PARC Y RHATH

• Rhymni

Coleg Brenhinol Cerdd a Drama Cymru

Cododd y Rhufeiniaid sawl caer yma o OC 55 i 400. Mae'r gorthwr o gyfnod y Normaniaid. William Burges, y pensaer, a gynlluniodd y prif adeiladau hardd yn niwedd y 19^{eg} ganrif. Rhoddodd teulu Bute y castell a'r parc i ddinas Caerdydd yn 1947.

• Parc Cathays

CASTELL CAERDYDD

• Stadiwm Principality

CANOL DINAS CAERDYDD

Cafodd dêl £1 miliwn gyntaf y byd ei harwyddo yma yn 1904.

CREU · GWIR · IN · THESE · STONES
FEL · GWYDR · HORIZONS
O · FFWRNAIS · AWEN · SING

Gallwch weld perfformiadau byw, ac aros yng Nghanolfan yr Urdd yma.

Cartref Cynulliad Cenedlaethol Cymru ers 2006.

Y Gyfnewidfa Lo
• Canolfan Mileniwm Cymru

Y Senedd

Hen ganolfan Cwmni Dociau Bute o 1897.

Adeilad y Pierhead
Yr Eglwys Norwyaidd

• Grangetown

Canolfan Iâ Cymru

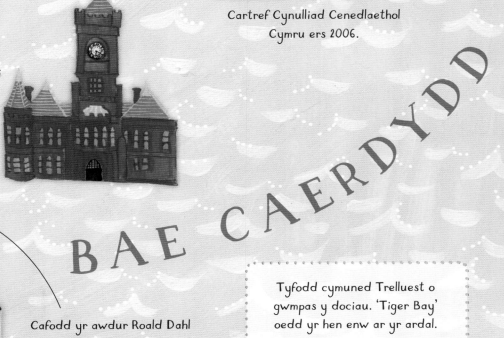

Canolfan Iâ Cymru yw cartref tîm hoci iâ Diafoliaid Caerdydd.

Cafodd yr awdur Roald Dahl ei fedyddio yma.

Tyfodd cymuned Trelluest o gwmpas y dociau. 'Tiger Bay' oedd yr hen enw ar yr ardal.

41

CAERFFILI

278 km² (107 milltir²)

TORFAEN

POWYS

BLAENAU GWENT

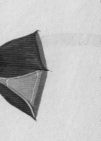

Gallwch fynd i weld Amgueddfa'r Tŷ Weindio yma. Roedd yr injan yn arfer codi'r caets a oedd yn mynd â glowyr Glofa Elliot i'r ffas lo.

Mae Pont Calzaghe yn dathlu camp Joe Calzaghe, pencampwr bocsio'r byd rhwng 1997 a 2009.

MYNYDD PEN-Y-FAN

AFON SIRHYWI

Mae modrwy Rufeinig 2,000 mlwydd oed yn yr amgueddfa hefyd.

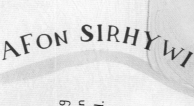

Glofa oedd yn arfer bod yma, ond parc hyfryd sydd yma nawr. O'r man uchaf, fe welwch chi 'Sultan, y merlyn pwll glo', y cerflun mwyaf ar wyneb y tir yn y DU.

Tredegar Newydd

• Bargod

Mae'r pêl-droediwr Aaron Ramsey yn dod o dref Caerffili. Aeth i Ysgol Gyfun Cwm Rhymni.

• Rhymni

AFON RHYMNI

Gallwch ymweld â'r maenordy a gafodd ei godi yn 1550. Mae'n amgueddfa fyw ac yn edrych fel y byddai yn 1645, pan ymwelodd y brenin Siarl I â'r lle. Mae actorion wedi'u gwisgo fel gweision yn rhoi hanes bywyd yn yr 17eg ganrif i chi.

MERTHYR

• Trecelyn

• Coed-duon

CAMLAS SIR FYNWY A BRYCHEINIOG

Rhisga •

• Machen

Mae model LEGO o gastell Caerffili yn Legoland Windsor.

Mae'r tŵr de-orllewinol yn gwyro mwy na Thŵr Pisa!

• Cwm-carn

AFON EBWY

Mae'r grŵp roc Manic Street Preachers yn dod o'r fan hon.

Roedd plwm a chopr yn arfer cael eu mwyngloddio yn yr ardal hon.

Bob diwedd mis Gorffennaf, mae Gŵyl y Caws Mawr yn cael ei chynnal, gydag 80,000 o bobl yn dod i fwynhau pob math o adloniant.

Mae caer Rufeinig wedi bod yma ers tua OC 75.

• Penallta

Ynys-ddu

Ar 14 Hydref 1913, cafodd 439 o ddynion a bechgyn eu lladd mewn ffrwydrad yng nglofa Universal. Dyma'r drychineb fwyaf yn hanes maes glo de Cymru. Mae Amgueddfa Treftadaeth Cwm Aber yn adrodd yr hanes.

Roedd glowyr yn hoff iawn o gaws gwyn Caerffili. Mae model o gosyn caws Caerffili ar gylchfan yn y dref.

Castell Caerffili yw'r mwyaf yng Nghymru, a'r ail fwyaf ym Mhrydain ar ôl castell Windsor. Mae'n ymestyn dros 12ha. Dechreuodd Gilbert de Clare y gwaith o'i godi yn 1268. Daeth y gwaith i ben am gyfnod yn 1270 pan ymosododd Llywelyn ap Gruffudd arno. Yn 1316, ceisiodd Llywelyn Bren gipio'r castell drwy ei roi o dan warchae gyda 10,000 o'i ddynion.

• Senghennydd

Caerffili •

CASTELL

MYNYDD CAERFFILI

• Llancaeach Fawr

Mae'n debyg bod llawer o ysbrydion yma, felly mae teithiau ysbrydion yn cael eu cynnal gyda'r nos.

Mae cerflun o Tommy Cooper, y digrifwr (1921–1984), gyferbyn â'r castell. Cafodd ei eni yng Nghaerffili.

Mae'r castell wedi cael ei ddefnyddio fel lleoliad i lawer o raglenni teledu a ffilmiau, gan gynnwys Dr Who.

Roedd dodrefn hardd
yn arfer cael eu
gwneud yma rhwng
1929 ac 1940.

BLAENAU GWENT
POBLOGAETH
TUA
69,600
★ ★ ★

FYNWY

Rasa

PARC CENEDLAETHOL
BANNAU BRYCHEINIOG

Gallwch chi wneud pob math o
weithgareddau awyr agored ym
Mharc Bryn Bach, gan gynnwys
canŵio, saethyddiaeth a dringo.

Bryn-mawr

Nant-y-glo

AFON SIRHYWI

Glynebwy

Tredegar

Mae Twr y Cloc (1858)
wedi'i wneud o haearn
bwrw o'r gwaith
haearn lleol.

Yn 1816, cododd Joseph Bailey,
y meistr haearn lleol, ddau dŵr
crwn. Roedd yn ofni bod ei
weithwyr yn mynd i wrthryfela.
Byddai ef a'i deulu wedi gallu
dianc i'r ddau 'gastell' i fyw.

Roedd gweithfeydd Cwmni Dur, Haearn
a Glo Glyn Ebwy yn arfer ymestyn am
5km ar hyd llawr y dyffryn. Roedd
34,000 o ddynion yn gweithio yno ar
ddechrau'r 20fed ganrif.

Ar ôl i'r gweithfeydd gau, daeth Gŵyl Gerddi
Cymru yma yn 1992. Erbyn hyn mae siopau a llawer
o weithgareddau eraill ym Mharc yr Ŵyl. Mae
gwarchodfa i dylluanod yn y parc, a gallwch fynd i
lawr y bryn ar y reid diwb hiraf ym Mhrydain!

EBWY FACH

Cwm

Mae llwybr
cerdded Ebwy
Fach yn mynd
rhwng dau lyn yng
Nghwm Tyleri.

Abertyleri

Cafodd Aneurin Bevan
(1897–1960), a sefydlodd y
Gwasanaeth Iechyd Gwladol,
ei eni yn Nhredegar.

Daw Pencampwyr Snwcer y
Byd, Ray Reardon a Mark
Williams, o'r ardal yma.

AFON EBWY

Six Bells

Aber-big

CAERFFILI

TORFAEN

BLAENAU GWENT

109 km² (42 milltir²)

Cafodd tai teras eu codi
i roi cartref i weithwyr
a'u teuluoedd.

Cafodd 45 o ddynion eu
lladd mewn damwain ym
mhwll glo Six Bells yn
1960. Ers 2010, mae cofeb
arbennig i gofio hyn.

Ar ddechrau'r 19^{eg} ganrif, roedd gweithfeydd haearn Blaenafon yn cynhyrchu mwy o haearn nag unrhyw le arall yng Nghymru.

PARC CENEDLAETHOL BANNAU BRYCHEINIOG

Blaenafon

Big Pit

Yn Amgueddfa Lofaol Big Pit gallwch fynd o dan ddaear i weld sut roedd glowyr yn arfer gweithio. Cafodd y pwll ei suddo yn 1860 ac roedd yn gweithio tan 1973.

Mae Tirlun Diwydiannol Blaenafon yn Safle Treftadaeth y Byd oherwydd mai yma mae'r olion gorau o waith haearn o ddiwedd y 18^{fed} ganrif.

TORFAEN
POBLOGAETH TUA
92,100
★ ★ ★

Abersychan

Pont-y-pŵl oedd un o'r trefi diwydiannol cynharaf yng Nghymru. Roedd gwaith haearn yma yn 1425.

Pont-y-pŵl

Ym Mharc Pont-y-pŵl mae Cell Meudwy neu Groto Cregyn, o'r 19g. Mae cregyn, esgyrn a dannedd anifeiliaid yn ei addurno.

CAMLAS SIR FYNWY A BRYCHEINIOG

Pant-teg

TorfAen
126 km² (49 milltir²)

'Tref newydd' a gafodd ei chodi yn 1950.

Cwmbrân

Mae stadiwm athletau yma.

CWM BRÂN

Pont-hir

BLAENAU

GWENT

CAERFFILI

SIR FYNWY

CASNEWYDD

CASNEWYDD

190 km² (73 milltir²)

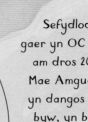

Mae caer a baddonau Rhufeinig Caerllion yn dangos sut byddai milwyr Rhufeinig yn hamddena yn yr 2il ganrif.

Ymosododd Owain Glyndŵr ar gastell Casnewydd yn 1402.

Mae Casnewydd yn ddinas ers 2002.

Sefydlodd y Rhufeiniaid gaer yn OC 75, a bu milwyr yma am dros 200 o flynyddoedd. Mae Amgueddfa Lleng Cymru yn dangos sut roedden nhw'n byw, yn brwydro, yn addoli ac yn marw.

CAERFFILI

Y Betws •

Mae murlun mosaig a choncrit yn dangos pa mor bwysig oedd y gamlas a'r rheilffordd i Gasnewydd yn y 19eg ganrif.

AFON EBWY

CAMLAS SIR FYNWY A BRYCHEINIOG

AFON WYSG

Yn Sgwâr Westgate, mae cerflun i gofio Gwrthryfel y Siartwyr yn 1839. Martsiodd 5,000 o Siartwyr arfog i Westy'r Westgate. Roedden nhw'n protestio dros yr hawl i bob dyn gael pleidlais. Cawson nhw eu trechu ar ôl brwydr 25 munud yn erbyn milwyr. Cafodd John Frost, yr arweinydd, ei alltudio i Van Diemen's Land, (Tasmania).

Tŷ-du •

CASTELL

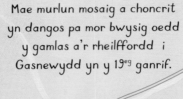

• Rodney Parade

CANOL DINAS CASNEWYDD

Basaleg •

Sefydlodd y sant Gwynllyw eglwys ar Stow Hill yn y 6ed ganrif. Yma mae Eglwys Gadeiriol Sant Gwynllyw heddiw.

Tŷ Tredegyr

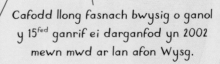

DOCIAU ALEXANDRA

M4   A48(M)

Cafodd llong fasnach bwysig o ganol y 15fed ganrif ei darganfod yn 2002 mewn mwd ar lan afon Wysg.

Beth am ymweld â Thŷ Tredegyr, cartref y teulu Morgan o 1660 i 1951? Mae'r gerddi a'r parc yn werth eu gweld hefyd.

CAERDYDD

46

ORFAEN

Buodd arweinwyr y byd yn aros yng Ngwesty'r Celtic Manor pan oedd uwchgynhadledd NATO yno yn 2014.

Cafodd cystadleuaeth golff bwysig, Cwpan Ryder, ei chynnal yng Nghasnewydd yn 2010.

Llanfaches

Pen-hw

CASNEWYDD
POBLOGAETH
TUA
147,800
★ ★ ★

• Caerllion

M4   • Celtic Manor

SIR FYNWY

Rodney Parade yw cartref clwb rygbi rhanbarthol y Dreigiau a chlwb pêl-droed Casnewydd.

RYGBI

Yn y 19^{eg} ganrif, roedd rhai pobl yn dweud mai yn Lloegr roedd Casnewydd.

• Liswerry

Mae cerflun y Don Ddur gan Peter Fink ar lan afon Wysg.

• Felodrom Cenedlaethol Cymru

Mae llawer o feicwyr enwog wedi ymarfer yn Felodrom Cenedlaethol Cymru.

Gallwch ddringo i fyny a thros y Bont Gludo, neu gael eich cludo mewn gondola. Cafodd ei chodi yn 1906.

refonnen

• Whitson

LLWYBR ARFORDIR CYMRU

Mae gwarchodfa natur Gwlyptir Casnewydd RSPB yn lle gwych i wylio adar a bywyd gwyllt a gweld hen oleudy Dwyrain Wysg.

Yn y 1830au, Casnewydd oedd prif borthladd allforio glo de Cymru.

MÔR HAFREN

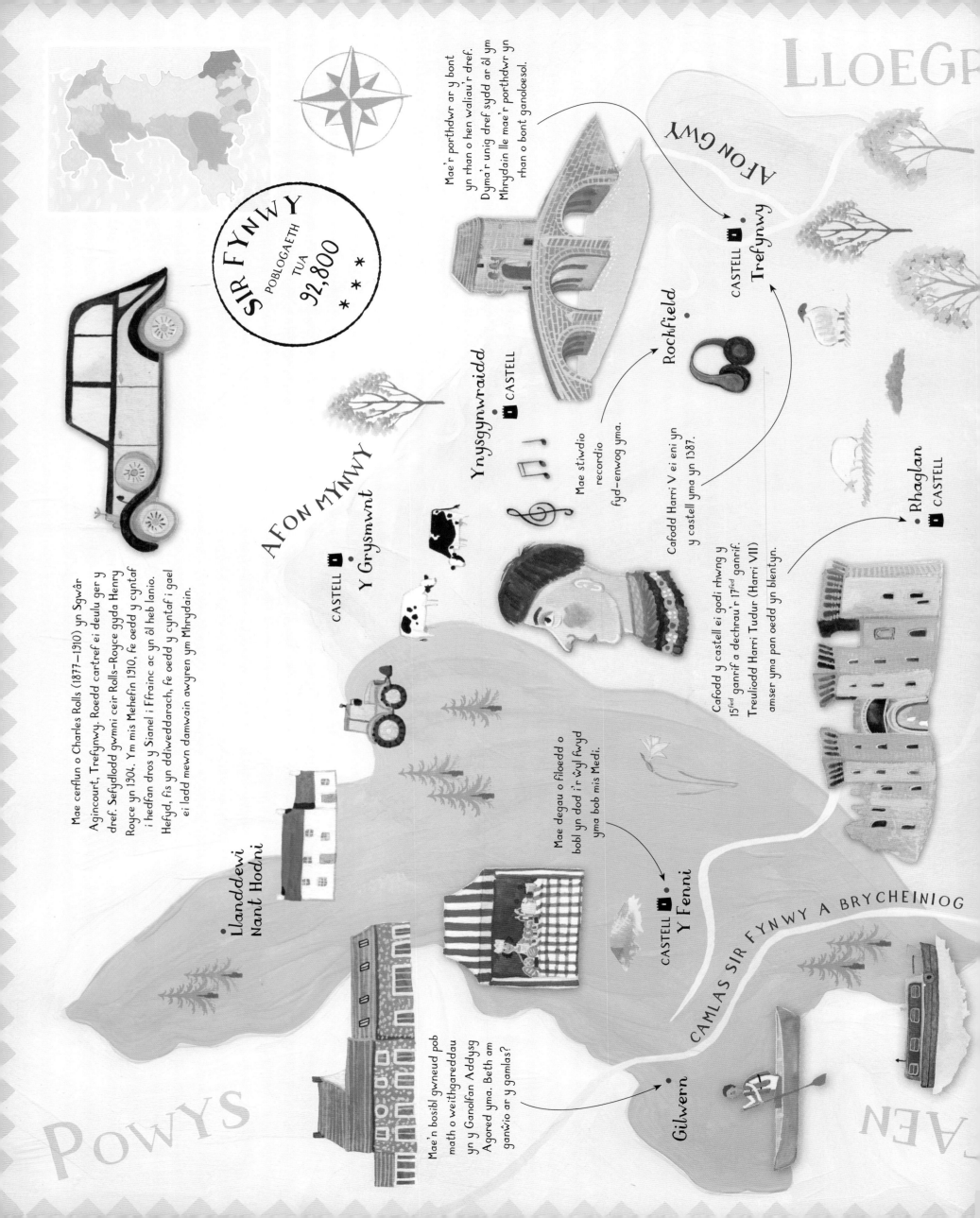

POWYS

AEN

SIR FYNWY
POBLOGAETH
TUA
92,800

AFON GWY

Mae'r porthdwr ar y bont yn rhan o hen waliau'r dref. Dyma'r unig dref sydd ar ôl ym Mhrydain lle mae'r porthdwr yn rhan o bont ganoloesol.

CASTELL • Trefynwy

Rockfield •

Mae stiwdio recordio fyd-enwog yma.

Cafodd Harri V ei eni yn y castell yma yn 1387.

Ynysgynwraidd • ■ CASTELL

Cafodd y castell ei godi rhwng y 15fed ganrif a dechrau'r 17fed ganrif. Treuliodd Harri Tudur (Harri VII) amser yma pan oedd yn blentyn.

• Rhaglan ■ CASTELL

AFON MYNWY

Mae cerflun o Charles Rolls (1877–1910) yn Sgwâr Agincourt, Trefynwy. Roedd cartref ei deulu ger y dref. Sefydlodd gwmni ceir Rolls–Royce gyda Henry Royce yn 1904. Ym mis Mehefin 1910, fe oedd y cyntaf i hedfan dros y Sianel i Ffrainc ac yn ôl heb lanio. Hefyd, fis yn ddiweddarach, fe oedd y cyntaf i gael ei ladd mewn damwain awyren ym Mhrydain.

CASTELL ■ Y Grysmwnt

Mae degau o filoedd o bobl yn dod i'r Ŵyl Fwyd yma bob mis Medi.

CASTELL ■ • Y Fenni

Llanddewi Nant Hodni •

Mae'n bosibl gwneud pob math o weithgareddau yn y Ganolfan Addysg Agored yma. Beth am ganŵio ar y gamlas?

Gilwern •

CAMLAS SIR FYNWY A BRYCHEINIOG

AFON GWY

• Abaty Tyndyrn

Cafodd abaty ei godi yma yn 1131. Roedd yn un o'r rhai mwyaf cyfoethog yng Nghymru.

Mae cwrs rasio ceffylau yma.

Cas-gwent • CASTELL

Pont Hafren

TWNNEL HAFREN

Ail Bont Hafren

• CASTELL CALDICOT

M4

M4

A48(M)

Caer-went •

Mae'r castell (1067) yn bwysig achos dyma'r adeilad hynaf yng Nghymru sydd ddim yn perthyn i'r eglwys. Yn 2013, cafodd pennod arbennig o Dr Who ei ffilmio yma i ddathlu bod y gyfres yn 50 oed.

Yn 1568, cafodd pres ei gynhyrchu am y tro cyntaf ym Mhrydain mewn ffowndri yn Nhyndyrn.

CASTELL ■ • Brynbuga

AFON WYSG

Collodd byddin Owain Glyndŵr lawer o filwyr ym Mrwydr Pwllmelyn yn 1405.

Cafodd Alfred Russel Wallace (1823–1913), y naturiaethwr enwog, ei eni yma.

CASNEWYDD

Gallwch weld waliau tref 5 metr o uchder o gyfnod y Rhufeiniaid (tua OC 180) yma.

Cafodd y bont gyntaf ei hagor yn 1966. Cyn hynny roedd ceir yn croesi afon Hafren ar fferi. Enillodd y bont lawer o wobrau am ei dyluniad. Mae'r ddau dŵr yn 123m o uchder.

Cafodd yr ail bont ei hagor yn 1996. Mae'n ymestyn 5km ar draws yr afon.

O 2018 ymlaen, does dim rhaid talu toll i groesi Pont Hafren.

SIR FYNWY

850 km² (330 milltir²)

MÔR HAFREN

LLOEGR

Cafodd 76,400,100 o frics eu defnyddio i adeiladu'r twnnel rheilffordd, sydd tua 7km o hyd. Teithiodd y trên cyntaf drwyddo yn 1885, a'r teithwyr cyntaf yn 1886. Am 100 mlynedd, dyma'r twnnel rheilffordd o dan ddŵr hiraf yn byd.

49

CHWEDLAU A THRADDODIADAU

Llanelwy
Dic Aberdaron, a fu'n crwydro Cymru a Lloegr yn droednoeth a'i wallt yn hir, yn cario telyn, llyfrau a chath. Roedd yn gallu siarad 14 o ieithoedd! Bu farw yn 1843, ac mae ei fedd yn Llanelwy.

GOGLEDD-DDWYRAIN CYMRU

Calan Mai – dawnsio, cario'r fedwen haf o gwmpas, a'r Cadi Haf yn casglu arian.

Rhita Gawr
Bu'n dwyn barfau brenhinoedd eraill Cymru a'u gwau i'w glogyn.

Dinas Emrys
Brwydr rhwng y ddraig goch a'r ddraig wen

Gelert
• **Beddgelert**

Yr Wyddfa

• **Bala**
Llyn Tegid

Pennant Melangell
Santes Melangell a'r Tywysog Brochwel

Os byddwch chi'n treulio'r nos yma, byddwch chi naill ai'n fardd neu'n wallgof pan fyddwch chi'n deffro.

• **Cadair Idris**

• **Pontarfynach**

Ceridwen y ddewines
Taliesin •

• **Caernarfon**

YNYS MÔN

Dyffryn Nantlle
Blodeuwedd

Nant Gwrtheyrn
Rhys a Meinir

PENRHYN LLŶN

Porthmadog
Madog ab Owain Gwynedd a aeth i America tua 1170.

• **Aber-soch**
Clustiau March ap Meirchion

CEREDIGION

Seiriol Wyn a Chybi Felyn

Breuddwyd Macsen

Trystan ac Esyllt

Aberdaron •

Ynys Enlli •

Mae rhai yn dweud bod y Brenin Arthur a'r dewin Myrddin wedi'u claddu yma.

MÔR IWERDDON

POWYS

Y Plygain

Caledfwlch, cleddyf y Brenin Arthur. Cafodd ei daflu i Lyn Llydaw ar yr Wyddfa.

Tregaron

Llanddewibrefi
Dewi Sant a'r bryn yn codi er mwyn i'r bobl ei weld.

Ystrad-ffin
Twm Siôn Cati

Myddfai
Meddygon Myddfai

Llyn y Fan Fach
Merch Llyn y Fan

Aberpennar
Guto Nyth Brân

Y Fari Lwyd

Dyffryn Aman
Y Twrch Trwyth

Llangynwyd

Ynysforgan

Llyfr Coch Hergest

Hen Ŵr Pencader

Pencader

Caerfyrddin
Hen dderwen Myrddin y dewin

Castellnewydd Emlyn

Gors-las
Llyn Llech Owain

Cydweli

'Hen Fenyw Fach Cydweli' a oedd yn gwerthu losin du.

Cantre'r Gwaelod

Gwiber Emlyn
Disgynnodd y Wiber i'r afon wedi; iddi gael ei saethu; gwenwynwyd yr afon gan y corff a lladdwyd yr holl bysgod.

Cwm Gwaun
Calennig

Pwyll, Pendefig Dyfed

Barti Ddu o Gasnewydd-bach

Arberth

BAE

Bendigeidfran

Drudwy Branwen

Gwales
Ynys oddi; ar arfordir Sir Benfro. Gwledd gyda phen Bendigeidfran.

MÔR HAFREN

51

Y Celfyddydau

Hedd Wyn a'r Gadair Ddu

Cafodd Hedd Wyn ei ladd cyn cael gwybod iddo ennill Cadair yr Eisteddfod Genedlaethol. Mae'n cael ei adnabod fel 'Bardd y Gadair Ddu'.

Gillian Clarke

Beirdd

Roedd bardd ym mhob llys pan oedd brenhinoedd a thywysogion gan Gymru. Roedd beirdd yn cael eu talu i gyfansoddi cerddi.

Y Prifardd Ceri Wyn Jones o Aberteifi yw Meuryn *Talwrn y Beirdd*, rhaglen ar Radio Cymru lle mae beirdd yn cystadlu. Fe sy'n penderfynu pa farciau y mae'r beirdd yn eu cael.

Mae Bardd Plant Cymru yn cael ei ddewis bob dwy flynedd.

Mae pobl ledled y byd yn mwynhau barddoniaeth Saesneg Dylan Thomas (1914–53), R. S. Thomas (1913–2000), Gillian Clarke ac Owen Sheers.

Mae barddoniaeth Gymraeg mewn cynghanedd yn unigryw. Patrymau o odl a chyflythreniad yw cynghanedd. Mae'r bardd sy'n ysgrifennu'r gerdd orau mewn cynghanedd yn yr Eisteddfod Genedlaethol yn ennill cadair ac yn cael y teitl 'prifardd'.

Y Prifardd Mererid Hopwood yw'r ferch gyntaf i ennill cadair yr Eisteddfod Genedlaethol.

Mererid Hopwood

Y Prifardd Ifor ap Glyn yw Bardd Cenedlaethol Cymru ers 2016.

R. S. Thomas

Eisteddfod yr Urdd yw gŵyl ieuenctid fwyaf Ewrop.

Arlunwyr

Mae arlunwyr enwog o Gymru'n cynnwys Syr Kyffin Williams (1918–2006) o Ynys Môn, Aneurin Jones (1930–2017) o Aberteifi, Josef Herman (1911–2000), a ddaeth i fyw i Ystradgynlais o Wlad Pwyl yn 1944, Charles Tunnicliffe (1901–79), a fu'n byw ar Ynys Môn, a'r brawd a'r chwaer Augustus John (1878–1961) a Gwen John (1876–1939) o Sir Benfro.

Daeth arlunwyr enwog fel J. M. W. Turner (1775–1851) i Gymru er mwyn peintio tirluniau.

Awduron

Mae Kate Roberts (1891–1985), yr awdur o Rosgadfan, Caernarfon, yn cael ei galw'n 'Frenhines ein llên'.

Mae awduron plant poblogaidd sy'n dod o Gymru'n cynnwys T. Llew Jones (1915–2009) a Roald Dahl (1916–90).

T. Llew Jones

Charles Tunnicliffe

Syr Kyffin Williams

Canolfan y Celfyddydau, Aberystwyth

Ble mae eich canolfan gelfyddydau leol chi? Mae'n lle da i weld sioe, cyngerdd, neu arddangosfa gelf.

Kate Roberts

Roald Dahl

Richard Burton

Actorion

Mae llawer o actorion ardderchog yn dod o Gymru. Mae rhai wedi dod yn sêr yn UDA hefyd, fel Matthew Rhys ac Ioan Gruffudd o Gaerdydd, a Syr Anthony Hopkins a Richard Burton (1925–84) o ardal Port Talbot. Mae Catherine Zeta-Jones, o Abertawe yn wreiddiol, wedi ennill Oscar am actio. Cafodd yr actor enwog Michael Sheen ei fagu ym Maglan.

Syr Anthony Hopkins

Canolfan Pontio, Bangor

Côr Meibion

Canu

'Gwlad y gân' yw Cymru, ac mae llawer o bobl yn mwynhau canu mewn corau.

Mae rhai cantorion o Gymru yn enwog ledled y byd.

Syr Bryn Terfel

Kizzy Crawford

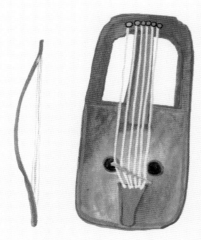

Y Fonesig Shirley Bassey

Catrin Finch

Syr Tom Jones

Y delyn yw offeryn cenedlaethol Cymru. Y delyn deires yw'r delyn draddodiadol Gymreig. Mae ganddi dair rhes o dannau. Mae Catrin Finch, o Geredigion yn wreiddiol, yn un o delynoresau gorau'r byd.

Hen offeryn Cymreig oedd y crwth. Roedd yn debyg i ffidil, yn cael ei chwarae â bwa, ond roedd ganddo chwe thant.

Mae grwpiau pop Cymraeg a Saesneg yng Nghymru.

Mae canu gwerin a cherdd dant (canu penillion gyda'r delyn) yn boblogaidd iawn.

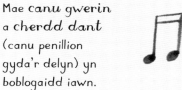

Manic Street Preachers

Cyfansoddwyr

Mae Syr Karl Jenkins, o Ben-clawdd, ger Abertawe, a William Mathias (1934–92) o Hendy-gwyn ar Daf, yn enwog dros y byd fel cyfansoddwyr.

Syr Karl Jenkins

William Mathias

Mae bandiau pres ym mhob rhan o Gymru, yn arbennig lle roedd pyllau glo, chwareli llechi neu weithfeydd haearn.

Mae dawnsio o bob math yn boblogaidd yng Nghymru: dawnsio disgo, dawnsio gwerin, a chlocsio. Mae rhai pobl yn dathlu Dydd Gŵyl Dewi drwy gael twmpath dawns.

Y Wisg Gymreig

Roedd Gwenynen Gwent (1802–96) yn byw ym Mhlasty Llanofer. Augusta Hall oedd ei henw iawn hi. Roedd diddordeb ganddi mewn cerddoriaeth a dawnsio gwerin Cymreig. Datblygodd hi'r wisg Gymreig.

ChwArAEon

Cafodd **rygbi** ei chwarae am y tro cyntaf yng Nghymru yng ngholegau Llanymddyfri a Llanbedr Pont Steffan tua 1850.

Neil Jenkins

Cafodd **Undeb Rygbi Cymru** ei sefydlu yn 1881. Erbyn hyn mae clybiau rygbi'r undeb a rygbi'r gynghrair dros y wlad i gyd.

Mae pedwar tîm rygbi rhanbarthol yng Nghymru: Scarlets Llanelli, Gweilch Abertawe Castell-nedd, Gleision Caerdydd a Dreigiau Gwent.

Bydd gemau rhyngwladol yn cael eu chwarae yn **Stadiwm Principality** yng Nghaerdydd.

Mae **Nigel Owens** yn dyfarnu gemau rygbi rhyngwladol pwysig.

Mae **rygbi merched** yn boblogaidd iawn. Mae tîm merched Cymru'n cystadlu yng Nghwpan y Byd.

Cyn dyddiau rygbi a phêl-droed, roedd **bando** a **chnapan** yn gemau poblogaidd.

Roedd **bando** yn debyg iawn i hoci, gyda ffon yn taro pêl. Roedd pobl yn ei chwarae mewn mannau fel y traeth sydd y tu ôl i waith dur Port Talbot heddiw.

Roedd **cnapan** yn fwy tebyg i rygbi. Y cnapan oedd y bêl bren, tua'r un maint â phêl griced. Roedd chwaraewyr yn cael rhedeg gyda'r cnapan, ei gicio a'i daflu. Weithiau roedd dau dîm o gannoedd o bobl yn chwarae gêm rhwng dau bentref.

Cnapan

Bando

Mae **syrffio**'n boblogaidd iawn yng Nghymru.

Mae **achub bywyd** o'r tonnau yn gamp bwysig, ac mae clybiau ar hyd yr arfordir.

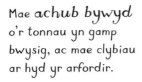

Mae Academi Hwylio Genedlaethol Cymru ym Mhlas Heli, Pwllheli.

Pêl-droed yw'r gamp fwyaf poblogaidd yng Nghymru. Cafodd Cymdeithas Bêl-droed Cymru ei sefydlu yn 1876.

Mae chwe thîm o Gymru'n chwarae mewn cynghreiriau yn Lloegr: Abertawe, Caerdydd, Casnewydd, Wrecsam, Bae Colwyn a Merthyr.

Mae 12 tîm yn chwarae yn Uwch Gynghrair Cymru.

Llwyddodd **tîm dynion** Cymru i gyrraedd rownd gynderfynol Euro 2016.

Mae **tîm menywod** Cymru'n cystadlu ar lefel ryngwladol hefyd.

Gareth Bale

Chris Coleman

Rheolwr tîm pêl-droed Cymru rhwng 2012 a 2017.

Mae **criced** yn cael ei chwarae yng Nghymru ers 1783. Cafodd clwb Morgannwg ei ffurfio yn 1888. Yn 1968, ar faes Sain Helen, Abertawe, trawodd Gary Sobers o India'r Gorllewin chwe rhediad chwe gwaith mewn un belawd. Fe oedd y cyntaf erioed i wneud hyn.

Cafodd math cynnar o **dennis** lawnt ei chwarae am y tro cyntaf yn Llanelidan, Sir Ddinbych, yn 1873.

Mae cartref tîm **hoci iâ** Diafoliaid Caerdydd yng Nghanolfan Iâ Cymru.

Aled Siôn Davies

Lyn Davies

Mae pencampwyr **athletau** Cymru yn cynnwys Colin Jackson yn y ras 110 metr dros y clwydi, Lyn Davies yn y naid hir, Y Fonesig Tanni Grey-Thompson yn rasio mewn cadair olwyn, ac Aled Siôn Davies mewn campau taflu Paralympaidd.

Mae clybiau **jiwdo** a **taekwon-do** ledled Cymru. Mae Jade Jones o'r Fflint wedi ennill medalau aur mewn taekwon-do yn y Gemau Olympaidd.

Jade Jones

Gallwch ddysgu **hwylio, canŵio** a **hwylfyrddio** ym Mhlas Menai, Canolfan Awyr Agored Genedlaethol Cymru.

Mae pobl yn canŵio, hwylio a rafftio dŵr ewynnog yn ardal y Bala. Mae'n bosibl rhwyfo ar rai afonydd yng Nghymru, ac ar y môr.

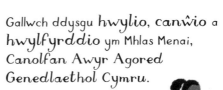

Mae cyrsiau **rasio ceffylau** yng Nghas-gwent, Ffos Las ger Trimsaran, Llanelli, a Bangor Is-coed ger Wrecsam.

Mae Cymru'n lle braf i **gerdded** gyda digon o lwybrau yn y mynyddoedd, yn y dyffrynnoedd ac ar hyd yr arfordir. Mae Llwybr Arfordir Cymru'n 870 milltir o hyd.

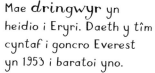

Mae **dringwyr** yn heidio i Eryri. Daeth y tîm cyntaf i goncro Everest yn 1953 i baratoi yno.

Enillodd y **nofiwr** a'r chwaraewr polo dŵr, Paulo Radmilovic o Gaerdydd, bedair medal aur mewn Gemau Olympaidd rhwng 1908 ac 1920.

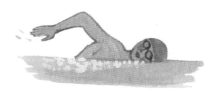

Mae ogofâu Cymru'n denu pobl sy'n hoffi **ogofa**.

Mae llawer o lwybrau beicio yng Nghymru. Y ddau lwybr hiraf yw'r **Llwybr Celtaidd** (220 milltir) o Aber-gwaun i Gas-gwent, a **Lôn Las Cymru** (257 milltir) o Gaerdydd i Gaergybi.

Mae ras **Velothon Cymru** yn digwydd am ddiwrnod ym mis Mehefin neu fis Gorffennaf.

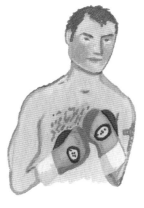

Nicole Cooke

Mae **beicio mynydd** yn boblogaidd ym mhob rhan o Gymru, mewn canolfannau fel Coed-y-brenin, ger Dolgellau.

Mae llawer o feicwyr enwog wedi ymarfer yn **Felodrom Cenedlaethol Cymru** yng Nghasnewydd.

Yn 2018, **Geraint Thomas** oedd y Cymro cyntaf i ennill y Tour de France.

Mae cyrsiau **golff** ar hyd a lled Cymru. Yn 2010, daeth cystadleuaeth Cwpan Ryder i ardal Casnewydd.

Mae sawl pencampwr **bocsio** wedi dod o Gymru, gan gynnwys **Joe Calzaghe** o Drecelyn ac **Enzo Maccarinelli** o Abertawe.

Johnny Owen

Joe Calzaghe

Mae **ralïo**'n boblogaidd iawn yng Nghymru, gyda llawer yn gyrru ac yn gwylio. Mae **Elfyn Evans** o Ddinas Mawddwy'n cystadlu ym Mhencampwriaeth Ralïo'r Byd.

Elfyn Evans

Mae llawer o Gymry'n hoffi chwarae neu wylio **snwcer**. Mae **Mark Williams** o Flaenau Gwent, **Matthew Stevens** o Gaerfyrddin, **Terry Griffiths** o Lanelli a **Ray Reardon** o Dredegar wedi bod yn bencampwyr y byd.

Mae **rasio ceir a beiciau modur** yn digwydd ar draciau fel Tŷ Croes, Ynys Môn, Pen-bre, Sir Gaerfyrddin a Llandŵ, Bro Morgannwg.

Yn Rhuthun, mae coflech i gofio am **Tom Pryce**, gyrrwr rasio talentog 27 oed a gafodd ei ladd yn Grand Prix De Affrica yn 1977.

Mae **dartiau**'n boblogaidd mewn cartrefi a thafarnau yng Nghymru.

Tom Pryce

BYD NATUR

Cewch wylio nythod gweilch y pysgod yng Ngwarchodfa Cors Dyfi ac ar lan afon Glaslyn ger Porthmadog.

Gwalch y pysgod

Y barcut coch yw aderyn cenedlaethol Cymru. Aeth yn brin iawn ar ddechrau'r 20fed ganrif. Erbyn hyn mae'n eithaf cyffredin. Gallwch fynd i'w gweld nhw'n cael eu bwydo mewn rhai mannau.

Gwarchodfeydd yr RSPB
Mae gan yr RSPB 11 gwarchodfa natur yng Nghymru. Maen nhw'n lleoedd gwych i wylio adar.

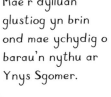

Mae miloedd lawer o huganod yn nythu ar Ynys Gwales, Sir Benfro.

Mae'r dylluan glustiog yn brin ond mae ychydig o barau'n nythu ar Ynys Sgomer.

Barcut coch

Yng Nghymru mae'r rhan fwyaf o'r brain coesgoch ym Mhrydain yn byw. Maen nhw'n bridio ar arfordir Sir Benfro, Ceredigion, Gwynedd, Ynys Môn a Gŵyr, ac yn Eryri hefyd.

Tylluan glustiog

Cŵn Cymreig

Mae cŵn defaid Cymreig yn fwy o faint na'r cŵn defaid arferol. Maen nhw'n gallu bod yn goch a gwyn, yn ddu a gwyn neu'n drilliw.

Cafodd y daeargi Cymreig ei fridio er mwyn hela anifeiliaid fel llygod a moch daear.

Mae dau fath o gorgi — Corgi Sir Benfro a Chorgi Ceredigion.

Afal Enlli
Hwn oedd afal prinnaf y byd yn 2000. Erbyn hyn mae pobl wedi tyfu rhagor o goed ac mae'n bosibl eu prynu.

Lili'r Wyddfa
Mae Lili'r Wyddfa'n tyfu yn Eryri, yr ardal lle mae mynyddoedd uchaf Cymru. Dyma'r unig fan ym Mhrydain lle mae hi'n tyfu.

Heboglys yr Wyddfa
Dyma un o blanhigion prinnaf y byd. Roedd pobl yn meddwl ei fod wedi diflannu yn y 1950au, ond cafodd ei weld eto yng Nghwm Idwal, Eryri, yn 2002.

Cenhinen Bedr Penfro

Lili'r dŵr
Ym mis Mehefin, mae lili'r dŵr yn garped hardd dros lynnoedd Bosherston yn Sir Benfro.

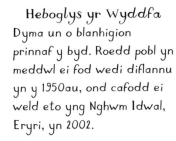

Gwyniad Llyn Tegid
Dyma'r pysgodyn mwyaf enwog yn llynnoedd Cymru. Mae'n byw yn Llyn Tegid, y Bala.

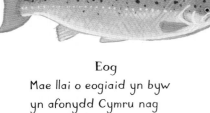

Eog
Mae llai o eogiaid yn byw yn afonydd Cymru nag oedd yn y gorffennol.

Anifeiliaid y môr

Heulforgi

Yr heulforgi yw'r anifail mwyaf yn y môr o gwmpas Cymru.

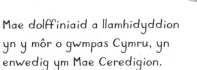

Dolffin

Mae dolffiniaid a llamhidyddion yn y môr o gwmpas Cymru, yn enwedig ym Mae Ceredigion.

Llamhidydd

Mae morloi llwyd i'w gweld ar hyd arfordir Sir Benfro a Phenrhyn Llŷn yn bennaf.

Mae hanner poblogaeth y byd o **adar drycin** Manaw yn bridio ar ynysoedd Sgomer a Sgogwm, Ynys Dewi ac Ynys Enlli.

Ardaloedd o Harddwch Naturiol Eithriadol

Mae pum ardal o harddwch naturiol eithriadol yng Nghymru:
· Ynys Môn
· Penrhyn Llŷn
· Penrhyn Gŵyr (yr un gyntaf yn y DU, yn 1956)
· Dyffryn Gwy
· Bryniau Clwyd a Dyffryn Dyfrdwy

Corsydd Teifi, Aberteifi

Lle da i weld glas y dorlan a dyfrgwn.

Daeth y Normaniaid â **chwningod** i Gymru yn yr 11eg a'r 12fed ganrif.

Mae rhai **ystlumod** prin yn byw yng Nghymru, fel yr **Ystlum Pedol Mwyaf**.

Mae cannoedd o **wiwerod coch** yn byw ar Ynys Môn. Dyma'r boblogaeth fwyaf yng Nghymru. Maen nhw i'w gweld hefyd yng Nghoedwig Clocaenog yn Sir Ddinbych, ac yng nghoedwigoedd canolbarth Cymru a phen uchaf Dyffryn Tywi.

Efallai y bydd pobl yn dod ag **afancod** 'nôl i Gymru. Diflannon nhw o Gymru yn y 15fed ganrif.

Pâl

Mae **palod** yn nythu ar Ynys Sgomer, Sir Benfro ac ar ynysoedd eraill y gorllewin a'r gogledd.

Ceirw

Y **carw coch** yw'r anifail gwyllt mwyaf yng Nghymru.

Mae llawer o geirw o'r enw **bwchadanas** yn byw mewn parciau fel Margam (Port Talbot) a Dinefwr (Llandeilo).

Mae pobl yn dweud bod llawer o **gathod mawr** yn crwydro'n wyllt yng Nghymru.

Bwchadanas

Mae **geifr gwyllt** yn crwydro yn Eryri, ar Benygogarth ger Llandudno, ar fynyddoedd yr Eifl ar Benrhyn Llŷn ac ar Gadair Idris ger Dolgellau.

Cafodd llawer o **goedwigoedd conwydd** eu tyfu yng Nghymru yn y 19eg a'r 20fed ganrif er mwyn cynhyrchu pren.

Ywen Llangernyw yw'r goeden hynaf yng Nghymru. Mae hi rhwng 4,000 a 5,000 o flynyddoedd oed.

Anifeiliaid y fferm

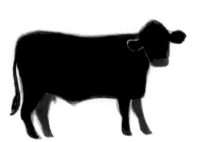

Gwartheg Duon Cymreig a Gwartheg Gwynion Parc Dinefwr — bridiau gwartheg arbennig o Gymru. Mae cyfreithiau Hywel Dda yn sôn am warlheg gwynion yn y 9fed ganrif.

Mae'r **Mochyn Cymreig** yn wyn, ac mae ei glustiau'n troi tuag i lawr.

Bridiau ceffyl o Gymru yw'r **Merlod Cymreig** a'r **Cobiau Cymreig**. Mae merlod ar fynyddoedd y Carneddau, yn Eryri, ers tua 500 CC.

Defaid yw'r anifeiliaid mwyaf cyffredin yng Nghymru. Mae llawer o fridiau o ddefaid Cymreig, gan gynnwys **Defaid Mynydd Cymreig, Defaid Llanwenog, a Defaid Llŷn**.

Sioe Amaethyddol Frenhinol Cymru

Mae ffermwyr ac ymwelwyr yn mwynhau Sioe Amaethyddol Frenhinol Cymru yn Llanelwedd bob mis Gorffennaf. Mae sioeau amaethyddol lleol yn cael eu cynnal dros Gymru i gyd.

BWYD

Gallwch fynd i **farchnad ffermwyr** yn eich ardal i brynu cynnyrch lleol.

Mae **caws** yn cael ei wneud ym mhob rhan o Gymru, bron. Beth yw eich caws lleol chi?

Mae'r Cymry bob amser wedi tyfu a bwyta **cennin**, mewn cawl a selsig Morgannwg.

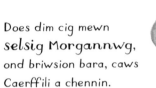

Does dim cig mewn **selsig Morgannwg**, ond briwsion bara, caws Caerffili a chennin.

Caws Caerffili
Roedd glowyr yn hoff i bwyta'r caws gwyn hwn.

Cymysgedd o gaws wedi'i doddi gyda llaeth, menyn neu wyau ar dost yw **caws pob**.

Mae **pice ar y maen** neu gacenni cri'n cael eu gwneud ar faen neu radell. Mae'r Cymry'n hoffi eu bwyta ers diwedd y 19eg ganrif.

Mae rhai cwmnïau bach yng Nghymru sy'n gwneud **siocledi, melysion** a **bisgedi** arbennig.

Roedd **bara brith** yn arfer cael ei bobi ar yr un diwrnod â bara cyffredin. Roedd siwgr, ffrwythau sych a sbeis yn cael eu rhoi yn y toes bara. Heddiw mae'n deisen fwy cyfoethog i'w bwyta amser te.

Gwymon arbennig wedi'i olchi, ei ferwi a'i dorri'n fân yw **bara lawr**. Roedd menywod yn gwneud hyn yn y 18fed a'r 19eg ganrif ar arfordir Sir Benfro, Ynys Môn a Gŵyr. Mae ffatri prosesu bara lawr ar Benrhyn Gŵyr heddiw.

Mae gwelyau **cregyn gleision Conwy** tua hanner milltir o'r dref, yn aber afon Conwy.

Mae pobl ardal Pen-clawdd yn casglu **cocos** o'r gwelyau ar aber afon Llwchwr ers canrifoedd. Menywod oedd yn arfer gwneud y gwaith hwn tra oedd y dynion yn gweithio fel glowyr yn y pyllau glo.

Mae **halen** o Ynys Môn yn cael ei allforio i dros 22 o wledydd ledled y byd.

Mae sawl cwmni yng Nghymru yn cynhyrchu **dŵr** potel.

Mae **Wisgi** Cymreig Penderyn, ger Hirwaun, wedi ennill gwobrau.

Daeth Eidalwyr draw i dde Cymru ar ddiwedd y 19eg ganrif i agor caffis. Mae caffis Eidalaidd yn gwerthu **hufen iâ** a **choffi** yn dal i fod yn boblogaidd heddiw.

Mae sawl hufenfa yng Nghymru. Maen nhw'n gwneud menyn, caws, hufen ac iogwrt o **laeth** neu **lefrith** lleol.

I wneud **cawl** neu **lobsgows**, rhaid berwi darnau o gig gyda darnau o datws a llysiau eraill fel moron a chennin.

Mae **cig oen Cymru** a **chig eidion Cymru** yn enwog drwy'r byd fel cigoedd blasus ac iach.

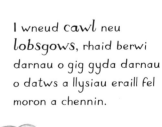

Tatws newydd cynnar Sir Benfro yw'r rhai cyntaf o Gymru yn y siopau. Mae hyn oherwydd hinsawdd fwyn y sir.

Mae **Ham Caerfyrddin** yn cael ei werthu yn y farchnad yno. Mae llawer o'r cogyddion gorau yn ei ddefnyddio.

Gofalu Am Ein Gwlad

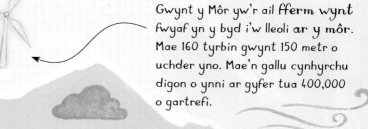

Gwynt y Môr yw'r ail fferm wynt fwyaf yn y byd i'w lleoli ar y môr. Mae 160 tyrbin gwynt 150 metr o uchder yno. Mae'n gallu cynhyrchu digon o ynni ar gyfer tua 400,000 o gartrefi.

Bydd **fferm solar** fwyaf Cymru yn cael ei hadeiladu yn Llanbadrig, Ynys Môn. Bydd hi'n cynhyrchu digon o ynni ar gyfer 15,500 o gartrefi'r flwyddyn. Hefyd, bydd ynni o'r fferm yn cael ei storio mewn batris.

Oes paneli solar, tyrbin gwynt neu bwmp gwres gan eich cartref neu'ch ysgol chi?

Does dim prinder **dŵr** yng Nghymru. Mae digon o ddŵr yn ein cronfeydd dŵr i bobl Cymru, a sawl ardal yn Lloegr hefyd. Ond mae'n bwysig i ni **beidio â gwastraffu dŵr.**

Mae Canolfan y Dechnoleg Amgen yn dangos sut gallwn fyw heb ddinistrio'r ddaear.

Cymru oedd un o'r gwledydd cyntaf ym Mhrydain i atal siopau rhag rhoi **bagiau plastig** am ddim, yn 2011. Mae'n bwysig atal plastig rhag llygru'r afonydd, y llynnoedd a'r môr.

Mae gan Gymru **Ardaloedd** Morol **Gwarchodedig** i wneud yn siŵr bod y môr yn lân a bod bywyd gwyllt yn iach.

Mae tri Pharc Cenedlaethol Cymru yn helpu i warchod yr amgylchedd.

Sut gallwn ni atal gwastraff a llygredd?
Cofiwch y pum pwynt:

- **Gwrthod** prynu cynnyrch os nad oes ei angen.
- **Lleihau** gwastraff drwy brynu'r hyn sydd ei angen yn unig.
- **Ailddefnyddio** popeth os yw'n bosibl.
- **Trwsio** neu gywiro pethau, yn lle eu taflu.
- **Ailgylchu** popeth sy'n amhosibl ei ailddefnyddio neu ei drwsio.

Mae **cerdded a seiclo** yn lle teithio yn y car yn helpu i atal llygredd. Mae rhannu ceir yn syniad da hefyd.

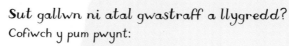

Mae ynni yn cael ei gynhyrchu o'r **llanw** yn Swnt Dewi, ger Tyddewi.

Mae llawer o ffermydd Cymru yn cynhyrchu **bwyd organig**, naturiol. Dydyn nhw ddim yn defnyddio pryfladdwyr sy'n gallu gwenwyno'r tir.

Bydd **ceir trydan** yn dod yn fwy poblogaidd yn y dyfodol. Maen nhw'n llawer glanach na cheir disel a phetrol.

Yng Nghymru, rydyn ni'n ceisio bod yn **gynaliadwy**. Mae hyn yn golygu ein bod ni'n gofalu am **adnoddau** Cymru a'r byd.

Os ydyn ni'n prynu bwyd sy'n cael ei gynhyrchu'n lleol, mae llai o **lygredd** achos bod dim angen ei gludo'n bell.

Ydy eich ysgol chi yn Eco-ysgol? Mae menter Eco-sgolion yn ceisio ysbrydoli disgyblion i ofalu am yr amgylchedd drwy ailgylchu, defnyddio llai o ynni, diffodd goleuadau ac ati.

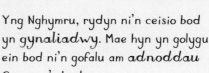

Mae **paneli solar** yn cael eu defnyddio i helpu i roi ynni i Ynys Echni, oddi ar arfordir Caerdydd. Maen nhw'n gallu cael eu dadrolio fel carped o drelar cyn pen dwy funud.

Cymru lân, Cymru lonydd – Cymru wen,
Cymru annwyl beunydd;
Cymru deg, cymer y dydd,
Gwlad y gân, gwêl dy gynnydd.

Môr o gân yw Cymru i gyd.
CEIRIOG (1832–1887)

TALIESIN O EIFION (1820–1876)

Gwisg genhinen yn dy gap,
A gwisg hi yn dy galon.

Pa wlad wedi'r siarad sydd
Mor lân â Chymru lonydd?
CALEDFRYN (1801–1869)

Cymru fach i mi –
Bro y llus a'r llynnoedd,
Corlan y mynyddoedd,
Hawdd ei charu hi.

EIFION WYN (1867–1926)

Arglwyddi, frodyr a chwiorydd, byddwch lawen a chedwch eich ffydd a'ch
cred, a gwnewch y pethau bychain a glywsoch ac a welsoch gennyf fi.

GEIRIAU O BREGETH OLAF
DEWI SANT (6ed ganrif)

PETHAU BYCHAIN

Siaradwch yn Gymraeg,
A chenwch yn Gymraeg,
Beth bynnag foch chwi'n wneuthur
Gwnewch bopeth yn Gymraeg.

MYNYDDOG (1833–1877)

Dyro eiriau drwy arwain, rho i bawb
air bach fesul cytsain
ac ymhob bro, byw y rhain
yw baich y pethau bychain.

ANEIRIN KARADOG (2016)

THE CHILDREN'S
ATLAS OF THE
HUMAN
BODY

ABERDEENSHIRE
BANCHORY ACADEMY
COUNCIL

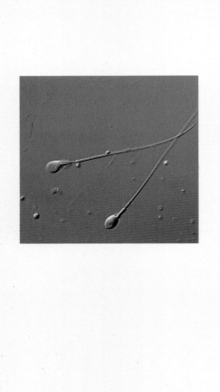
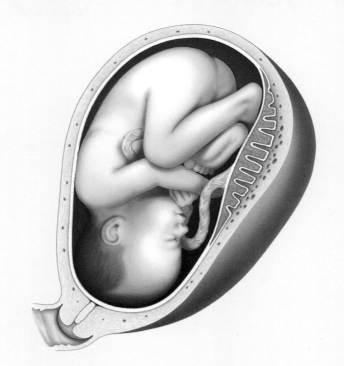
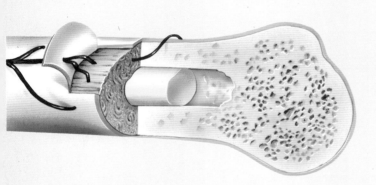
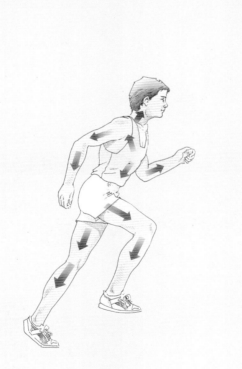

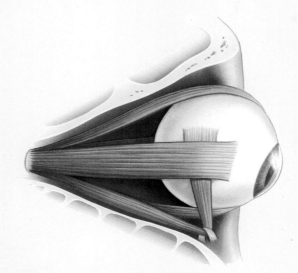

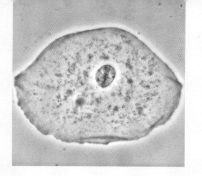

THE CHILDREN'S
ATLAS OF THE
HUMAN
BODY

ACTUAL SIZE BONES, MUSCLES AND
ORGANS IN FULL COLOUR

RICHARD WALKER

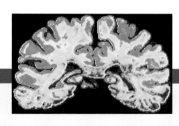

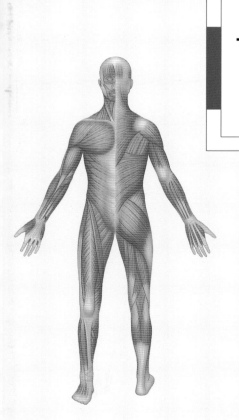

THE
APPLE
PRESS

ABERDEENSHIRE
BANCHORY ACADEMY
COUNCIL

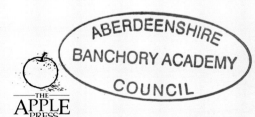

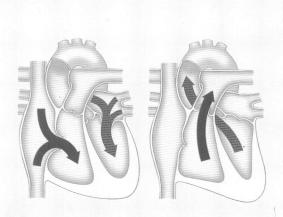

A QUARTO BOOK

Published in the UK by
The Apple Press
6 Blundell Street
London N7 9BH

Copyright © 1994 Quarto Children's Books Ltd

All rights reserved. No part of this publication may be reproduced,
stored in a retrieval system or transmitted in any form or by any means,
electronic, mechanical, photocopying, recording or otherwise,
without the permission of the copyright holder.

ISBN 1-85076-557-X

This book was produced by:
Quarto Children's Books Ltd
The Fitzpatrick Building
188–194 York Way
London N7 9QP

Managing Editor: Christine Hatt
Editors: Nigel Cawthorne
Designer: Graham Davis
Illustrators: Michael Courtney, Chris Forsey, Rob Shone;
Frank Kennard (poster)
Photographer: Paul Forrester
Picture research: Sarah Risely

Manufactured by Bright Arts (Pte) Ltd, Singapore.
Printed by Star Standard Industries (Pte) Ltd, Singapore.

Contents

Life-size human anatomy chart

Humans

Congratulations! You belong to an exclusive club with over five and a half thousand million members worldwide. That club is the human species, *Homo sapiens*. By looking at any of your fellow members, you can see immediately that they, like you, are human, whichever city, country, island or continent they may come from. But look closer. They may appear similar, but you can also tell these humans apart. Differences in outward appearance help you recognize family, friends and the famous. They will belong to one of two sexes – male or female. They may also be tall or short, have light or dark skin, be thin or fat. But despite these slight variations you can identify them as humans first and individuals second.

Under the skin

How does a car work? You cannot really tell just by looking at the outside. You need to get under the bonnet, look at the parts of the engine and see how they fit together.

The same applies to the human body. Looking from the outside, all you can see is an outer covering of skin. Even looking into the mouth and down the throat does not tell you very much. But under this outer layer lies a collection of different parts that collaborate to produce the complex organism called the human being.

The Children's Atlas of the Human Body gets under the skin, looks at all these vital body parts and explains clearly what they do and how they work together.

In the small intestine, food is digested and absorbed. In the large intestine waste material is transported out of the body (see pages 32-33).

The femur, or thigh bone, is the longest bone in the body. As part of the skeleton it helps support the body's weight (see pages 14-15).

The femoral artery carries oxygen-rich blood to all parts of the leg (see pages 20-21).

When an egg is fertilized by a sperm, it grows and develops into a baby inside the uterus (see pages 52-55).

The cerebrum is the control centre for all body activities (see pages 36-37).

The scapula, or shoulder blade, is the part of the skeleton where the humerus, or upper arm bone, attaches to the body (see pages 14-15).

The kidney filters waste out of the blood and sends it on its way out of the body in the form of urine (see pages 34-35).

Below the back of the cerebrum lies the cerebellum which ensures that all body movements are smooth and co-ordinated (see pages 36-37).

The spinal cord connects the brain with the rest of the body (see pages 38-39).

Inside the lung, life-giving oxygen is taken into the bloodstream in exchange for the waste product carbon dioxide (see pages 24-27).

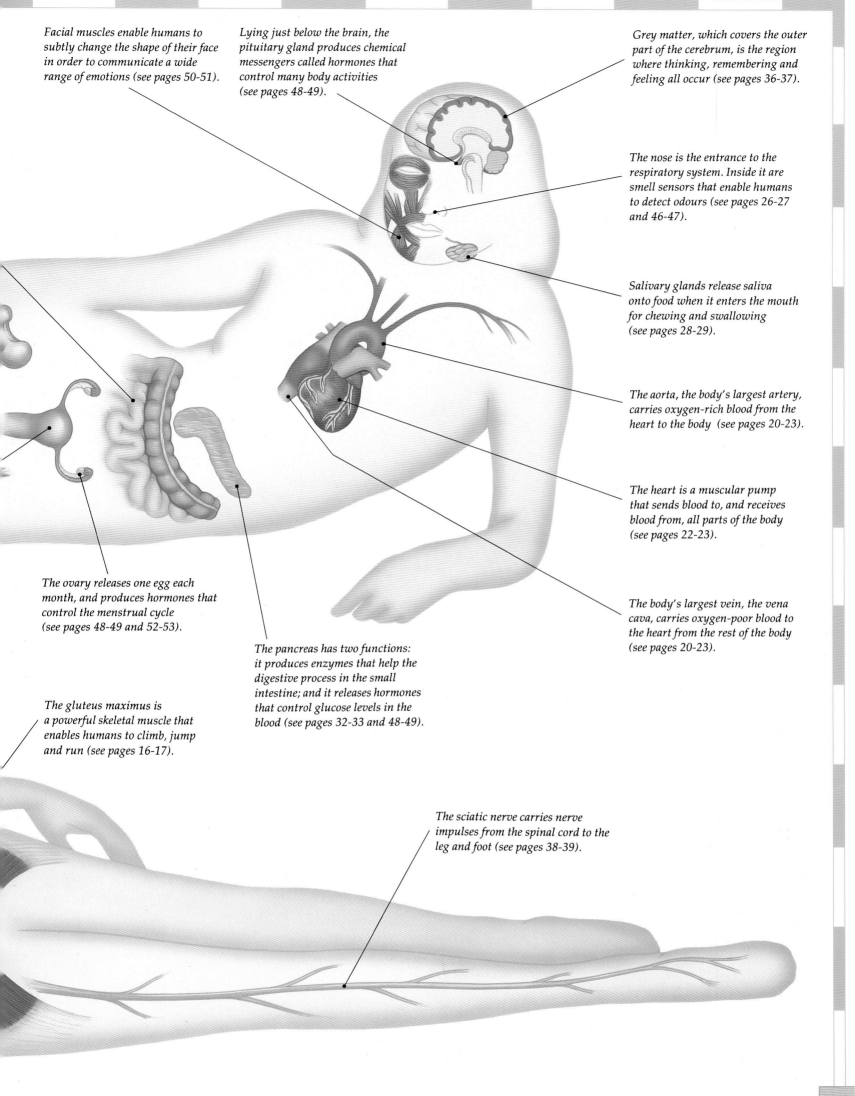

Facial muscles enable humans to subtly change the shape of their face in order to communicate a wide range of emotions (see pages 50-51).

Lying just below the brain, the pituitary gland produces chemical messengers called hormones that control many body activities (see pages 48-49).

Grey matter, which covers the outer part of the cerebrum, is the region where thinking, remembering and feeling all occur (see pages 36-37).

The nose is the entrance to the respiratory system. Inside it are smell sensors that enable humans to detect odours (see pages 26-27 and 46-47).

Salivary glands release saliva onto food when it enters the mouth for chewing and swallowing (see pages 28-29).

The aorta, the body's largest artery, carries oxygen-rich blood from the heart to the body (see pages 20-23).

The heart is a muscular pump that sends blood to, and receives blood from, all parts of the body (see pages 22-23).

The ovary releases one egg each month, and produces hormones that control the menstrual cycle (see pages 48-49 and 52-53).

The pancreas has two functions: it produces enzymes that help the digestive process in the small intestine; and it releases hormones that control glucose levels in the blood (see pages 32-33 and 48-49).

The gluteus maximus is a powerful skeletal muscle that enables humans to climb, jump and run (see pages 16-17).

The body's largest vein, the vena cava, carries oxygen-poor blood to the heart from the rest of the body (see pages 20-23).

The sciatic nerve carries nerve impulses from the spinal cord to the leg and foot (see pages 38-39).

Body systems

Think about someone kicking a football. The muscles pull on the leg bones to produce the kicking movement. In order to pull, muscles need energy. This is supplied, in the form of food and oxygen, by the bloodstream. The food is absorbed into the body through the intestines. The oxygen is absorbed through the lungs. Waste material produced by this body activity is removed via the lungs and the urine. And all of this is controlled by messages sent along the nervous system and by chemicals called hormones released into the bloodstream.

Just this one activity illustrates most of the body's systems at work. These major systems support the body, move it, control its activities, transport materials around it, remove waste from it, supply it with oxygen and food, and enable it to reproduce itself. Each has its job to do, but all work together in a co-ordinated way to produce the intricate complexity of the living human body.

Body systems work together rather like the parts of a city. The brain and the nervous system are the city council and telecommunication system. The digestive system provides food, like the shops and supermarkets. The blood system acts like a road network. And the body, like the city, needs to dispose of its waste.

BODYTOWN

City – body

Administration – brain

Food distribution – digestive system

Roads – bloodstream

Telephone exchange – nervous system

Waste disposal – urinary system

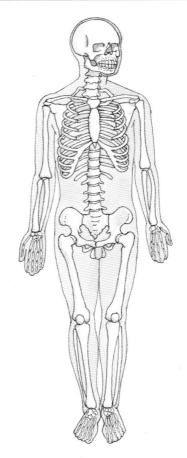

SKELETAL SYSTEM
The skeleton's 206 bones support the body, providing a flexible frame-work that is moved by muscles. Some protect delicate organs.

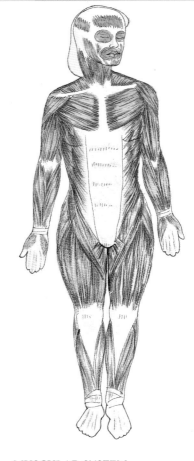

MUSCULAR SYSTEM
Over 600 muscles move the body by pulling bones. Other types of muscle are found in body organs such as the heart and bladder.

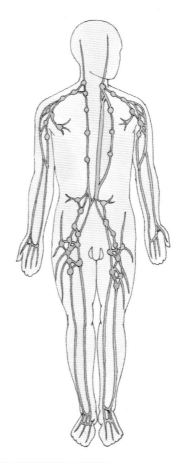

LYMPHATIC SYSTEM
A system of tubes collects fluid leaking from blood vessels, and drains it back into the blood. Lymph nodes filter out any harmful germs.

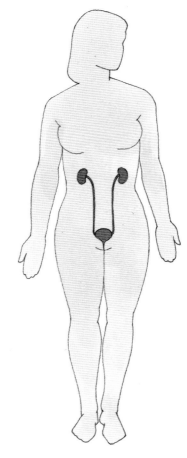

URINARY SYSTEM
Two kidneys filter the blood, removing waste and excess water. The product, urine, is stored in the bladder before release from the body.

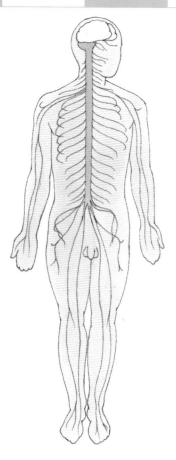

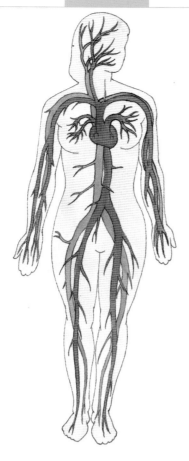

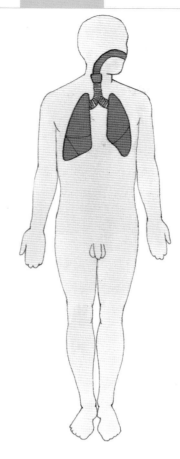

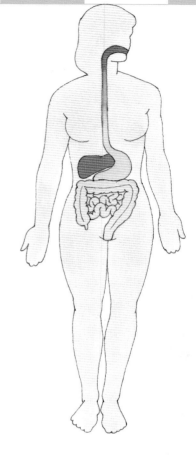

NERVOUS SYSTEM
This rapid response system co-ordinates body activities. Its control centre, the brain, receives and sends out messages along the nerves.

CIRCULATORY SYSTEM
The heart pumps blood around a network of blood vessels. This supplies all body parts with oxygen and food, and removes waste.

RESPIRATORY SYSTEM
The respiratory system extracts oxygen from air breathed into the lungs, exchanging it for carbon dioxide, which is breathed out.

DIGESTIVE SYSTEM
Food is needed for growth and repair, and to provide energy. The digestive system breaks down food and absorbs it, so it can be used.

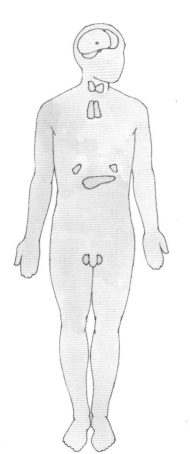

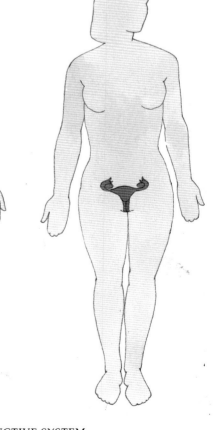

HORMONAL SYSTEM
Hormones, produced by endocrine glands (shown), control many body processes. Nervous and hormonal systems work closely together.

REPRODUCTIVE SYSTEM
The job of the reproductive system is to produce children. The male testes produce sperm which fertilize eggs produced in the female's ovaries.

11

Building blocks

The body's building blocks are called cells. However, unlike the building blocks of a house, bricks, cells are too small to see individually. Even the tiniest dot you can make with a pen is much bigger than the biggest of your body's cells and your body is made up of over a million million of them.

Each one of these cells is a single living unit. It contains all the instructions it needs to construct another cell just like it. It has the means to manufacture most of the materials it needs and ways of importing those it cannot. It has the capacity to eject waste products and the ability to generate the energy it needs to power all its activities. And cells do not work alone. They have ways of acting in concert with their neighbours. So when you put them all together, you get a walking, talking human being – just like you.

Mitochondrion – releases energy to power cell activities

Nucleus – controls cell activities

Lysosome – contains digestive chemicals used to break down and recycle worn-out parts of the cell

Ribosome – makes important chemicals called proteins

Golgi body – processes proteins, preparing some for export

THE CELL AS A COUNTRY
The components of a cell are like the parts of a country. The nucleus is the government. The mitochondria are the power stations. The endoplasmic reticulum is the road network. The ribosomes are the factories. And the outer membrane is the country's border with its customs posts.

Cell membrane – outer boundary which allows certain substances to pass in or out of the cell

INSIDE THE CELL
Cells may be small, but they are not simple. Each is packed with tiny components called organelles. Controlled by the nucleus, the organelles work together to keep the cell alive and working properly.

Centrioles – involved in cell division

Cytoplasm – liquid part of cell in which all other parts are suspended

THE MASTER MOLECULE
Inside the nucleus are long molecules that resemble twisted ladders. These are DNA molecules and contain, in code, all the information needed to construct and run a living cell.

TYPES OF CELL

Most of the body's billions of cells do not look like the 'typical' cell (below left), although they contain the same components. What a cell looks like depends on what it does.

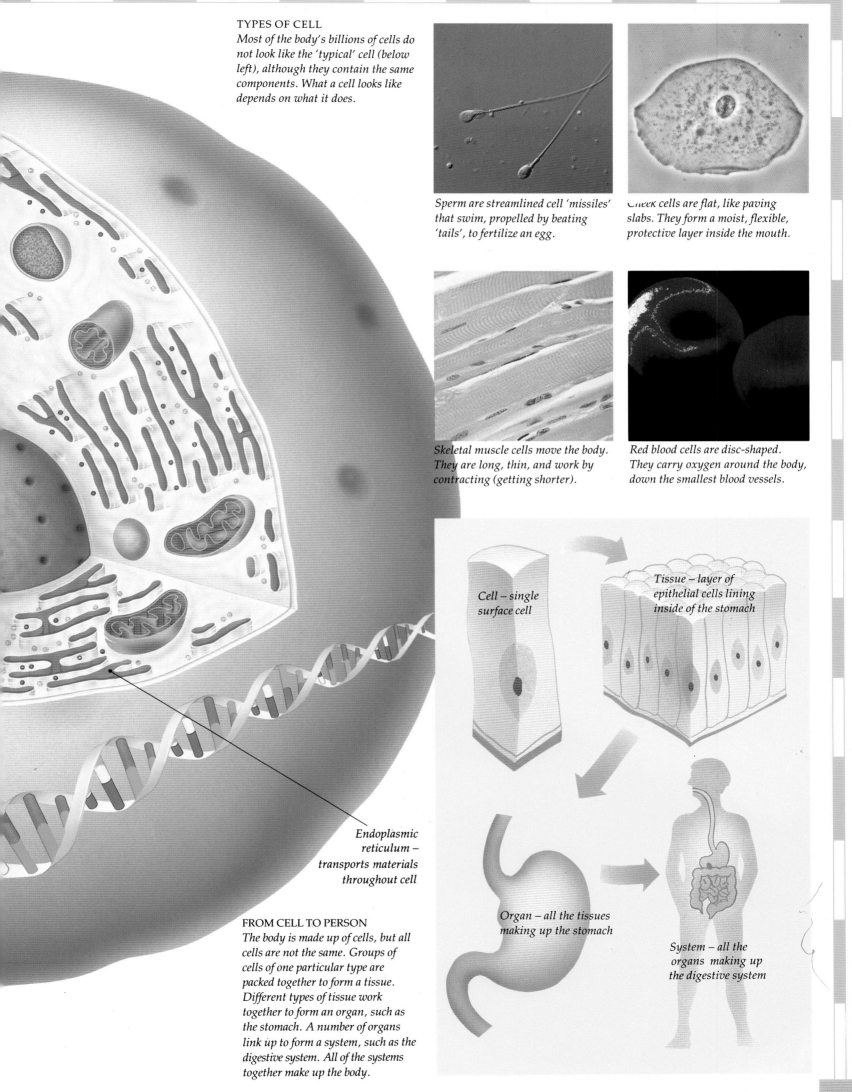

Sperm are streamlined cell 'missiles' that swim, propelled by beating 'tails', to fertilize an egg.

Cheek cells are flat, like paving slabs. They form a moist, flexible, protective layer inside the mouth.

Skeletal muscle cells move the body. They are long, thin, and work by contracting (getting shorter).

Red blood cells are disc-shaped. They carry oxygen around the body, down the smallest blood vessels.

Endoplasmic reticulum – transports materials throughout cell

Cell – single surface cell

Tissue – layer of epithelial cells lining inside of the stomach

Organ – all the tissues making up the stomach

System – all the organs making up the digestive system

FROM CELL TO PERSON

The body is made up of cells, but all cells are not the same. Groups of cells of one particular type are packed together to form a tissue. Different types of tissue work together to form an organ, such as the stomach. A number of organs link up to form a system, such as the digestive system. All of the systems together make up the body.

Skeleton

The word skeleton comes from the ancient Greek for 'dried up body' – not a very good description for the living, engineering marvel that supports and shapes you. Your skeleton is made up of 206 bones which are linked together to form a strong, but light, supporting framework. And bones are alive. The hard outside is made of tough fibres, minerals such as calcium and living cells with their own supply of blood and nerves.

But, the skeleton is much more than a support system. Bones provide an anchorage for muscles, allowing us to stand, walk, jump and run. Some bones, like the skull and ribs, protect delicate organs such as the brain and heart. The network of bones in your hands, which contains a quarter of the bones in your body, enables you to perform delicate movements like writing or sewing. The inner core of bones, the soft marrow, produces millions of blood cells each day.

INSIDE A BONE
Look inside a bone and you will see that it is not solid. The shaft is hollow, filled with bone marrow, and the end of the bone is honeycombed with spaces. This makes the bone both strong and light. Bone is six times stronger than a steel bar of the same weight.

FROM SKULL TO TOE BONE
The skull, backbone and ribcage form the central core of the skeleton. Fixed to the backbone are the shoulder and hip bones. The arm bones are attached to the shoulder bones, and the leg bones are attached to the hip bones. All bones are held together by tough straps of fibrous tissue called ligaments.

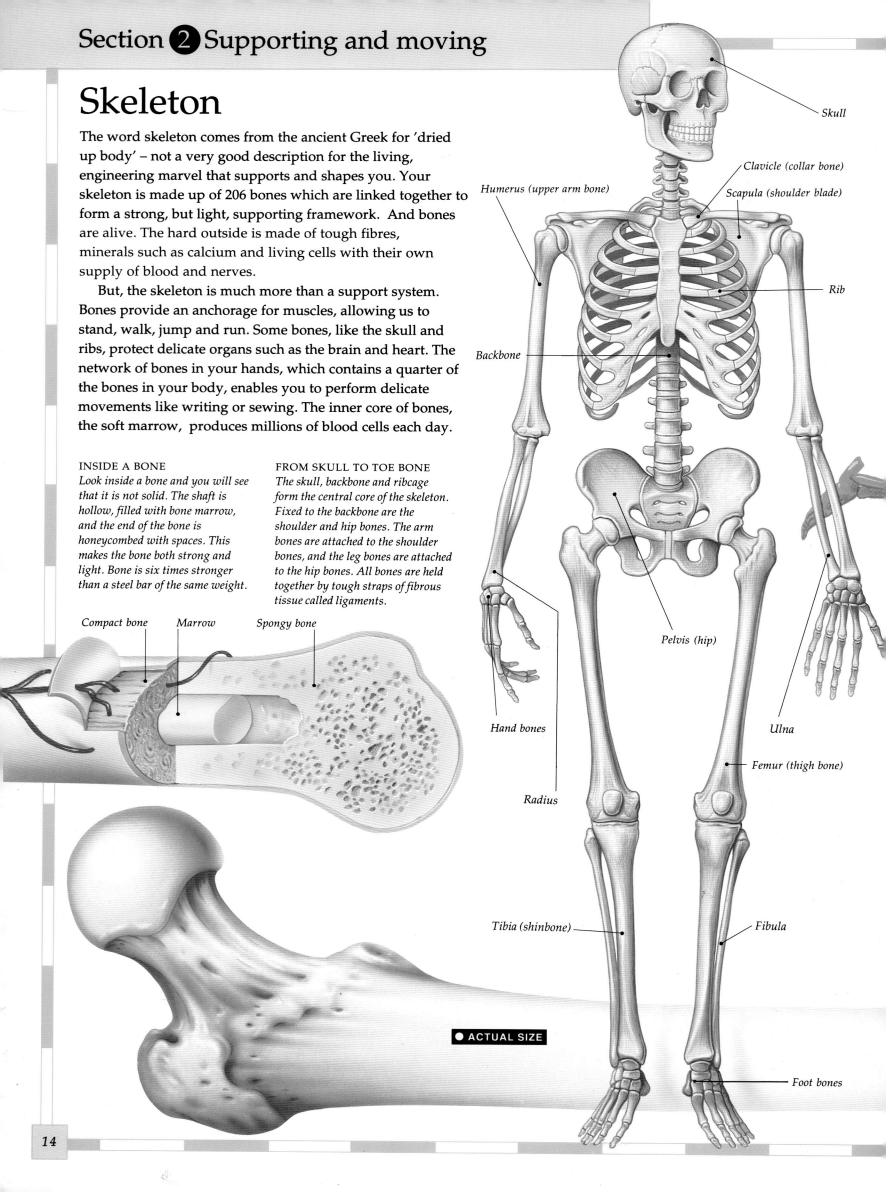

Compact bone   Marrow   Spongy bone

Skull

Clavicle (collar bone)

Scapula (shoulder blade)

Humerus (upper arm bone)

Rib

Backbone

Pelvis (hip)

Hand bones

Ulna

Radius

Femur (thigh bone)

Tibia (shinbone)

Fibula

Foot bones

● ACTUAL SIZE

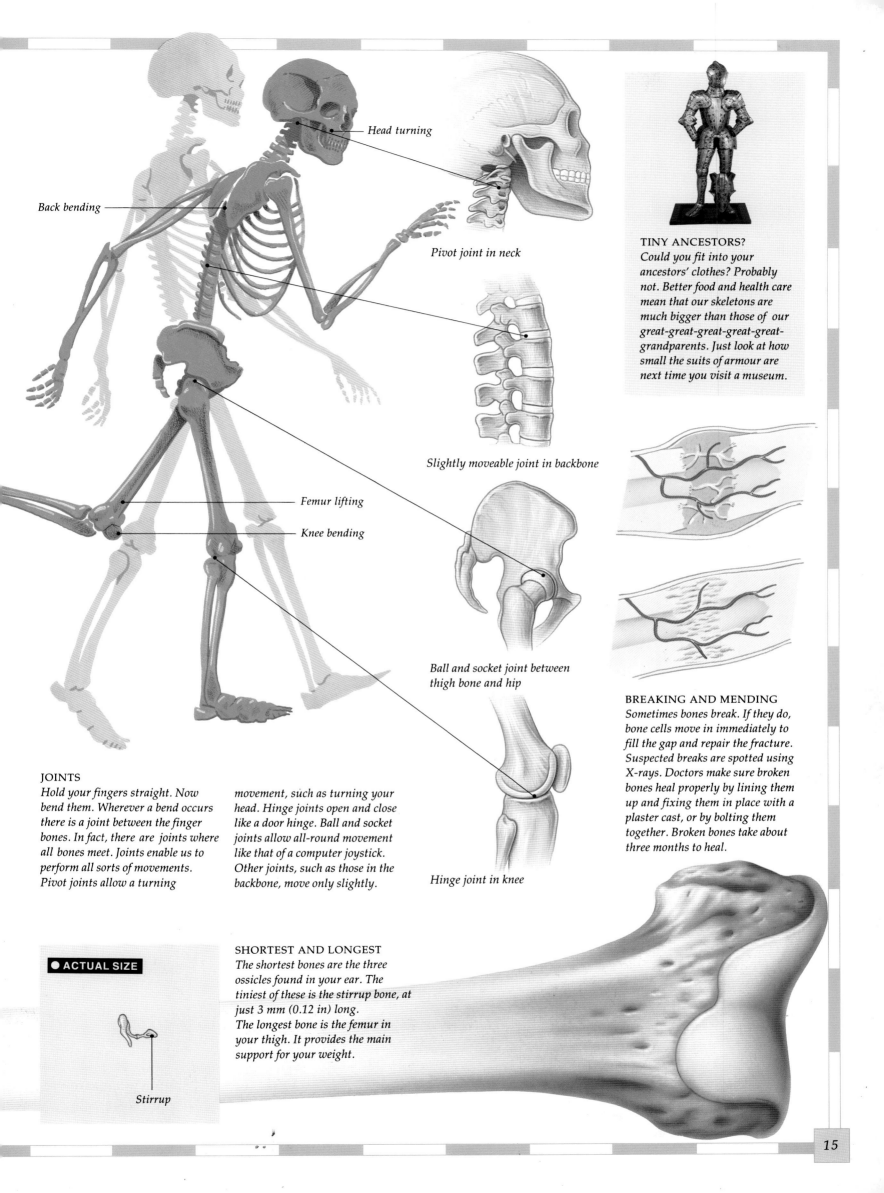

Head turning

Pivot joint in neck

Back bending

TINY ANCESTORS?
Could you fit into your ancestors' clothes? Probably not. Better food and health care mean that our skeletons are much bigger than those of our great-great-great-great-great-grandparents. Just look at how small the suits of armour are next time you visit a museum.

Slightly moveable joint in backbone

Femur lifting

Knee bending

Ball and socket joint between thigh bone and hip

BREAKING AND MENDING
Sometimes bones break. If they do, bone cells move in immediately to fill the gap and repair the fracture. Suspected breaks are spotted using X-rays. Doctors make sure broken bones heal properly by lining them up and fixing them in place with a plaster cast, or by bolting them together. Broken bones take about three months to heal.

JOINTS
Hold your fingers straight. Now bend them. Wherever a bend occurs there is a joint between the finger bones. In fact, there are joints where all bones meet. Joints enable us to perform all sorts of movements. Pivot joints allow a turning movement, such as turning your head. Hinge joints open and close like a door hinge. Ball and socket joints allow all-round movement like that of a computer joystick. Other joints, such as those in the backbone, move only slightly.

Hinge joint in knee

● ACTUAL SIZE

Stirrup

SHORTEST AND LONGEST
The shortest bones are the three ossicles found in your ear. The tiniest of these is the stirrup bone, at just 3 mm (0.12 in) long. The longest bone is the femur in your thigh. It provides the main support for your weight.

Muscles

Muscles make movement. A dancer's pirouette, the change in the size of your pupils, an artist's brush strokes, your heartbeat, swallowing food, breathing, or running a marathon – all are caused by muscles. Muscles work by pulling and are made up of cells that can contract (get shorter). Contraction requires energy, and energy release requires a constant supply of food and oxygen. This explains why, when muscles are working hard during exercise, your heart rate speeds up, increasing blood flow so that more food and oxygen are supplied to the muscles.

The muscles you are most aware of are skeletal muscles, the ones that move your body. Skeletal muscles are firmly linked to bones by tough, inelastic tendons. These muscles are under voluntary control – that is, they do what they are told. When they receive a message from the brain, they contract and pull on the bones they are attached to. Other types of muscle work automatically, whether you are asleep or awake. These are the involuntary muscles and are found in the intestines, bladder and other parts of the body. The brain tells them what to do without your being aware of it. Another type of involuntary muscle in the heart makes it beat by itself.

TEAM WORK
The muscles that move your skeleton work in pairs. The reason for this is simple. Muscles pull, but they cannot push. To bend the arm, for example, the biceps muscle pulls the forearm up. To straighten the arm, the biceps' team mate, the triceps, pulls the forearm down. Feel this for yourself. Your upper arm muscles get fatter as they pull, or contract, and thinner as they relax.

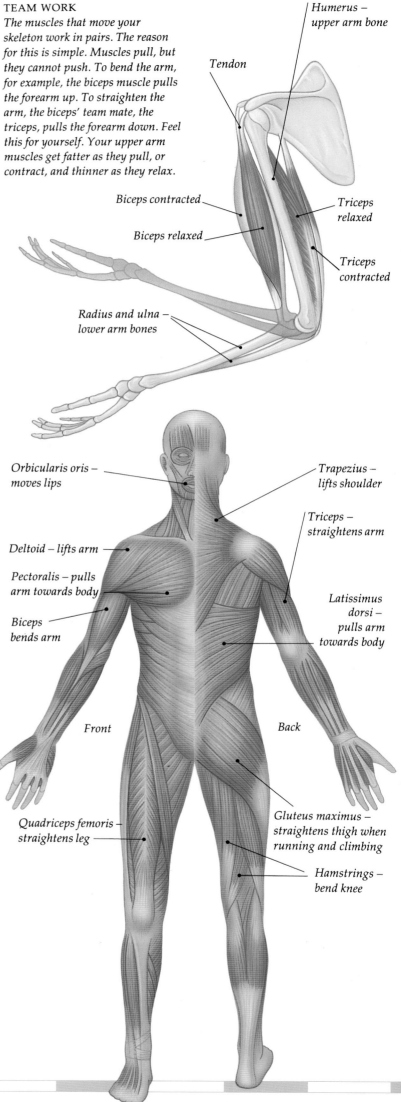

Humerus – upper arm bone

Tendon

Biceps contracted

Biceps relaxed

Triceps relaxed

Triceps contracted

Radius and ulna – lower arm bones

Orbicularis oris – moves lips

Deltoid – lifts arm

Pectoralis – pulls arm towards body

Biceps bends arm

Trapezius – lifts shoulder

Triceps – straightens arm

Latissimus dorsi – pulls arm towards body

Front

Back

Quadriceps femoris – straightens leg

Gluteus maximus – straightens thigh when running and climbing

Hamstrings – bend knee

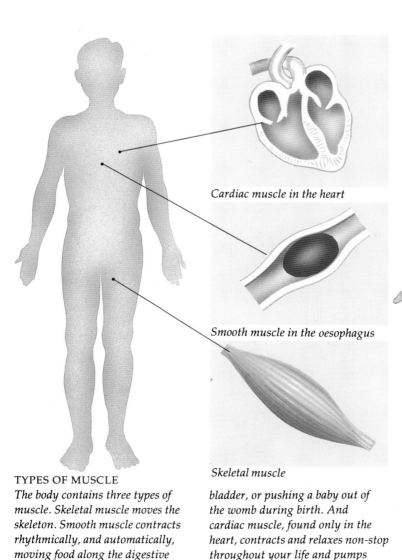

Cardiac muscle in the heart

Smooth muscle in the oesophagus

Skeletal muscle

TYPES OF MUSCLE
The body contains three types of muscle. Skeletal muscle moves the skeleton. Smooth muscle contracts rhythmically, and automatically, moving food along the digestive system, squeezing urine out of the bladder, or pushing a baby out of the womb during birth. And cardiac muscle, found only in the heart, contracts and relaxes non-stop throughout your life and pumps blood around your body.

MUSCLES IN ACTION
Put your finger in your mouth and bite it – but not too hard! The pain you feel is caused by the massive squeezing power of the masseter and temporalis muscles (right). Both are attached to the skull, at one end, and the lower jaw at the other. When they contract, the jaws and teeth clamp shut around food, enabling you to tear off chunks. To feel them contract, press your fingers just below the cheek bones and clench your teeth.

MAJOR MUSCLES
There are around 640 skeletal muscles in the body. The biggest is the gluteus maximus in the buttocks and thighs. The tiniest is the stapedius in the ear, which is just over 1 mm (0.04 in) long. Some major muscles are shown here (left). Each muscle moves a specific part of the body. Which muscle contracts when, and with what force, is co-ordinated by the brain. This is why we are able to walk, sit, stand, dance, run, write, paint, sculpt or juggle.

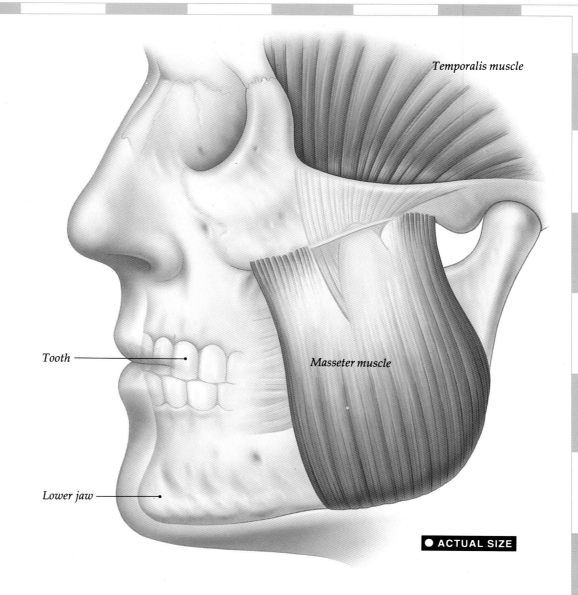

Temporalis muscle

Tooth

Masseter muscle

Lower jaw

● ACTUAL SIZE

INSIDE A SKELETAL MUSCLE
Like any other tissue in the body, muscles are made up of cells. But muscle cells, or fibres, are rather special. First, they are very long and thin, up to 30 cm (12 in) long. Second, they can shorten by up to a third of their length when stimulated by a nerve. The parts of the fibres that get shorter are the myofibrils. A bundle of myofibrils runs along the length of each fibre. They also give the fibre a stripy appearance – skeletal muscle is sometimes called striped muscle. The fibres themselves run along the length of the muscle and are, in turn, bundled together in fascicles. Bundles of fascicles make up the whole muscle. In all, over 2 000 fibres can make up a single muscle.

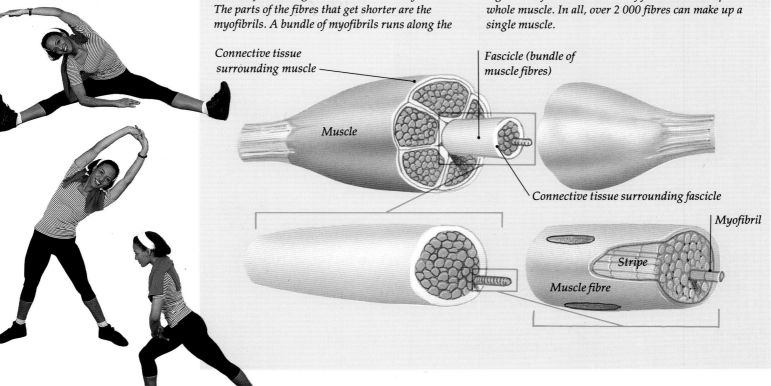

Connective tissue surrounding muscle

Fascicle (bundle of muscle fibres)

Muscle

Connective tissue surrounding fascicle

Myofibril

Stripe

Muscle fibre

Blood

Blood looks like simple red liquid, but it is much more than that. It is a complex mixture of cells floating in a watery solution, which itself contains many other substances. Most of these cells are the red blood cells that give blood its colour. There are over 25 million million of these in the blood. They are produced at the rate of 3 million per second by bone marrow. Each red blood cell survives for about four months. Red blood cells carry out one of the blood's major functions – carrying oxygen from the lungs to the rest of the body. But blood has many other jobs to do. It transports carbon dioxide and other wastes away from cells, ready to be disposed of. It supplies cells with food absorbed from the intestines. It carries chemical messengers called hormones. And its white blood cells fight off infection.

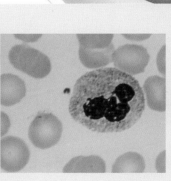

CELLS AND PLASMA
Blood is the body's only liquid tissue. Over half of it (55%) consists of a pale yellow liquid called plasma that lets blood flow. The rest (45%) is made up of red and white blood cells.

Plasma

Blood cells

IN THE BLOODSTREAM
Imagine you have shrunk until you are tiny enough to swim along a blood capillary. What would you see on your journey? Carried along by the flow you would bounce off the doughnut-shaped red blood cells that take up most of the space. On closer inspection, they look more orange than red. But look out for

smaller objects shaped like potato crisps. They are the platelets and are vitally important in stopping bleeding if you are cut. Don't stay too long in the bloodstream, though. One of the white blood cells may eat you. After all, inside the body, you would be considered to be a dangerous invader!

Neutrophil (white blood cell)

GIVING BLOOD
Sometimes, people lose so much blood through injury that their lives are at risk. But they can be saved by a blood transfusion. Other people's blood is transferred into their bloodstream.

The blood needed for transfusions is given, or donated, at special centres (above). However, before a donor gives blood, their blood group must be checked. Each person belongs to one of four blood groups.

These are the groups A, B, AB, and O. If blood from one group is given to a person of another group it can make them very ill. If they are dangerously ill already, giving them a transfusion of the wrong type of blood could kill them.

Giving blood takes about half an hour. During that time about 600 ml (1 pint) of blood is taken. This is stored in a blood bank until it is needed.

TYPES OF BLOOD CELLS

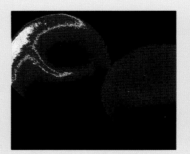

Red blood cells are dimpled discs with no nucleus. They are packed with orange haemoglobin, which picks up oxygen in the lungs and unloads it in the tissues – losing some of its bright colour.

Neutrophils are the most numerous white blood cells, with one for every thousand red blood cells. Neutrophils are hunters, seeking out and eating any invading germs.

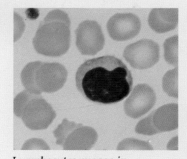

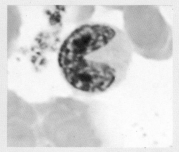

Lymphocytes engage in chemical warfare, producing antibodies that wipe out bacteria and viruses. There is one of these white blood cells for every 2 000 red ones.

Monocytes are the scourge of any germs invading the body's tissues. These white cells – there is one of these for every 10 000 red cells – hunt and eat all 'foreign' particles.

FIGHTING INFECTION

Every second of every day, the body is under attack from the bacteria and viruses that enter the body through the nose and throat, or through cuts in the skin, or in food. Fortunately, the body has two lines of defence to thwart any invaders. First, white blood cells, like the macrophage, (below) wander through the body's tissues searching relentlessly for any germs. Once discovered, harmful micro-organisms are surrounded, eaten and digested. Second, other white blood cells, called lymphocytes, produce killer chemicals, called antibodies, that identify and wipe out bacteria and viruses wherever they may be.

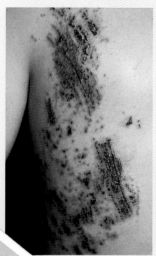

PREVENTING LEAKS

What happens if a pipe bursts at home? All the water leaks out. The same thing could happen if you cut yourself and a blood vessel breaks. Fortunately, the body has an automatic system to plug leaks as soon as they happen. This prevents you bleeding to death.

Plugging leaks works like this. At the site of the wound, a mesh of fibres forms a plug by trapping red blood cells like fish in a fishing net. This plug dries out to form a scab (left) that keeps germs out while the skin is repairing itself underneath.

Bacteria

White blood cell about to engulf, and eat, bacteria

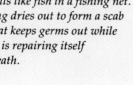

Platelet

Lymphocyte (white blood cell)

Red blood cell

Wall of blood capillary

Plasma

HOW MUCH BLOOD?

How many soft drink cans would your blood fill? If you are an adult female, between 12 and 15, depending on your size. If you are an adult male, you could fill between 15 and 18 cans.

Monocyte (white blood cell)

Blood vessels

Blood vessels are the highways of the body. The major roads are the big arteries and veins that carry blood between heart and body organs. The minor roads are the small arteries and veins that spread out through the tissues. The back alleys and driveways are the capillaries, along which the blood makes its deliveries to, and collections from, the individual cells. To see how the parts of this system fit together, let us follow the journey of a single red blood cell.

This blood cell has just been pumped, with millions of its companions, from the left side of the heart. It travels down the main artery, the aorta, into one of the many smaller arterial branches. These supply the organs, such as the liver and kidneys. Inside the organ the artery branches again and again until, eventually, the blood cell finds itself inside a capillary, which is just wider than the blood cell itself. Now our blood cell begins its return journey, squeezing along capillaries which join to form smaller veins which, in turn, join to form larger veins. Finally, our blood cell enters the right side of the heart through the vena cava, the biggest vein of all. After a detour to the lungs to pick up oxygen, the blood cell sets off for another trip around the circuit.

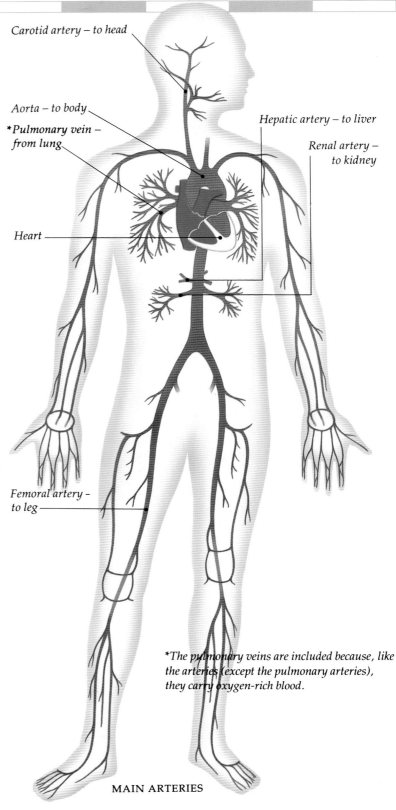

Carotid artery – to head

Aorta – to body

*Pulmonary vein – from lung

Heart

Hepatic artery – to liver

Renal artery – to kidney

Femoral artery – to leg

*The pulmonary veins are included because, like the arteries (except the pulmonary arteries), they carry oxygen-rich blood.

MAIN ARTERIES

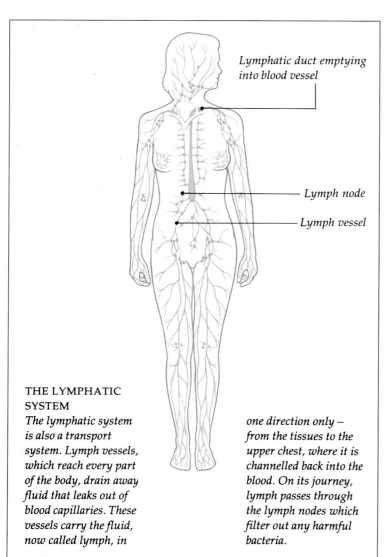

Lymphatic duct emptying into blood vessel

Lymph node

Lymph vessel

THE LYMPHATIC SYSTEM

The lymphatic system is also a transport system. Lymph vessels, which reach every part of the body, drain away fluid that leaks out of blood capillaries. These vessels carry the fluid, now called lymph, in one direction only – from the tissues to the upper chest, where it is channelled back into the blood. On its journey, lymph passes through the lymph nodes which filter out any harmful bacteria.

LARGEST ARTERY AND VEIN

Mightiest of all arteries is the aorta, the trunk route for blood pumped out of the left side of the heart. It is 2.5 cm (1 in) wide – about 2 500 times wider than the smallest capillaries. Its thick walls resist the high pressures generated by each heart beat. The largest vein, the vena cava, carries blood into the right side of the heart. In fact, there are two venae cavae, one from the upper part of the body, and one from the lower part. Although each vena cava is about as wide as the aorta, its wall is much thinner.

Vena cava

Aorta

● ACTUAL SIZE

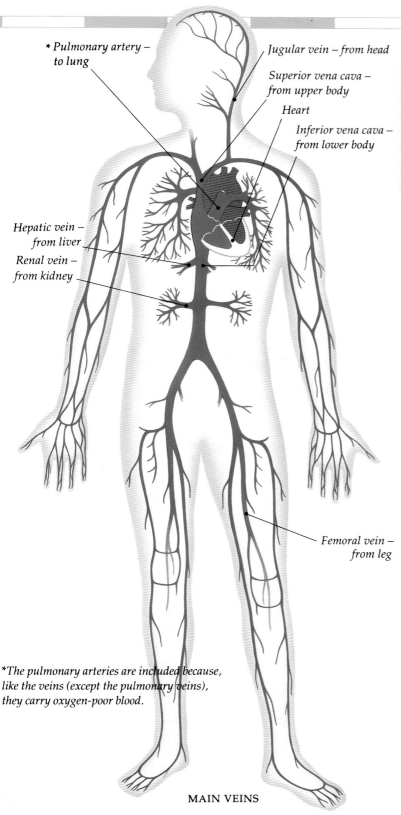

* Pulmonary artery – to lung

Jugular vein – from head

Superior vena cava – from upper body

Heart

Inferior vena cava – from lower body

Hepatic vein – from liver

Renal vein – from kidney

Femoral vein – from leg

*The pulmonary arteries are included because, like the veins (except the pulmonary veins), they carry oxygen-poor blood.

MAIN VEINS

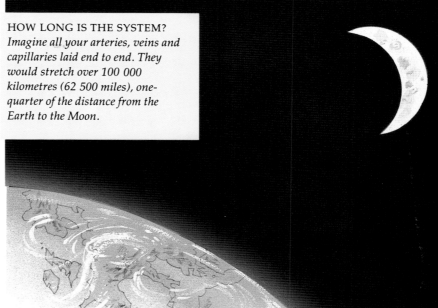

HOW LONG IS THE SYSTEM?

Imagine all your arteries, veins and capillaries laid end to end. They would stretch over 100 000 kilometres (62 500 miles), one-quarter of the distance from the Earth to the Moon.

ARTERIES

Arteries carry blood away from the heart. Apart from the pulmonary artery, which takes oxygen-poor blood to the lungs, they all transport oxygen-rich blood. Arteries have tough, thick walls that are both muscular and elastic. These strong walls ensure that arteries do not burst under the high pressure produced by the heart. The largest arteries are as wide as your thumb. The smallest, the arterioles, are no thicker than a piece of thread.

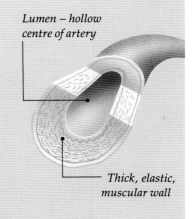

Lumen – hollow centre of artery

Thick, elastic, muscular wall

VEINS

Wall of vein, thinner and less muscular than artery

Veins carry blood towards the heart. Apart from the pulmonary vein which carries oxygen-rich blood from the lungs, all veins transport oxygen-poor blood. Veins have valves, to stop blood flowing backwards. Their walls are thin because veins are less likely to burst than arteries. The blood inside them is at a lower pressure. Veins range in diameter from around 2.5 cm (1 in) to that of a fine thread. The tiniest veins are called venules.

Valve

Lumen – hollow centre of vein

CAPILLARIES

Capillaries link arteries and veins. They are tiny, with diameters just big enough to allow red blood cells to pass along them in single file. The wall of a capillary is just one cell thick. Capillary networks form the point of contact between the blood system and body cells. As blood travels through the tissues, along the capillaries, materials such as food and oxygen are supplied to cells, while wastes and other products are removed.

Wall of capillary, one cell thick

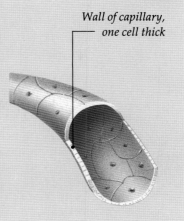

LIFE PULSE

Every time the heart contracts, it pushes blood along the arteries. Being elastic, arteries deal with these surges of blood by expanding, then shrinking. This movement is called a pulse. It tells how fast the heart is beating. You can feel your pulse wherever an artery is near the skin's surface. Find the pulse in your wrist (right). Now walk around. The pulse rate will go up as your heart beats faster.

At rest your pulse rate should be 60-80 beats per minute.

Heart

Why do we talk about broken hearts, or tugging at the heart strings, and draw arrows through hearts when people fall in love? Well, at one time, it was believed that the heart was the centre for feelings of love and emotion. We now know that emotions are controlled by the brain, and that the heart is simply a pump that pushes blood around every part of the body. But it is a resilient pump. The cardiac muscle that makes up the heart contracts around 75 times a minute, day and night, sometimes for over 100 years. It beats automatically, without instructions from the brain, only speeding up, or slowing down, with the body's demands. The heart maintains a constant flow of blood to every cell in the body. Without the unceasing supply of food and oxygen that the blood brings, the cells would die.

WHERE IS THE HEART?
The heart lies just left of centre in the chest cavity, or thorax, between the lungs. A bony cage, formed by the ribs and breastbone, surrounds and protects both heart and lungs.

OUTSIDE THE HEART
From the outside, the heart looks only slightly like the pink 'heart shape' seen on Valentine's cards. Clearly visible on its surface are the coronary arteries and veins, which supply the food and oxygen needed by heart muscle to maintain its non-stop pumping.

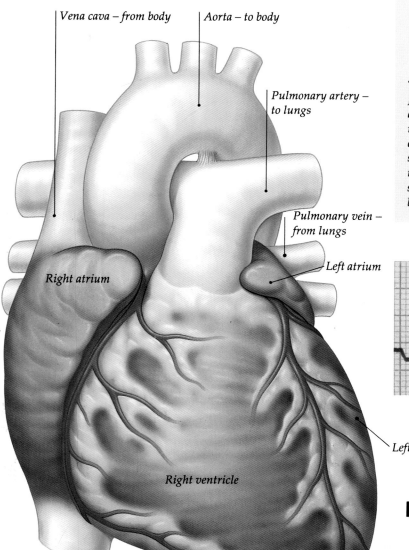

Vena cava – from body *Aorta – to body*

Pulmonary artery – to lungs

Pulmonary vein – from lungs

Left atrium

Right atrium

Left ventricle

Right ventricle

Lungs

Pulmonary artery

Pulmonary vein

Vena cava

Aorta

Heart

Capillaries in body tissues

THE BODY'S HIGHWAYS
Just as a country needs road and rail systems to supply its needs, so the body requires its own transport system to service its billions of cells. In the body, this is the circulatory system, a massive network of blood vessels that carries blood everywhere. At its core is the heart. This tireless pump sends blood to the lungs, where it picks up oxygen. Then it sends the blood around the rest of the body, supplying and nurturing the body's cells on its way.

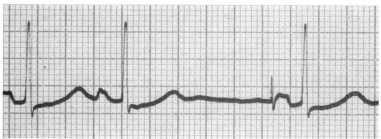

● ACTUAL SIZE

HEART TRACES
As the heart beats, an electric current passes right over its surface. This can be picked up by electrodes on the skin, producing a graph, or trace, called an ECG (electrocardiogram). By looking at an ECG, a doctor can tell whether the heart is working properly.

INSIDE THE HEART

The heart has two sides, the left and the right. Each side is divided into two chambers, the upper and the lower. The upper chambers, or atria, have thin walls. They pump blood into the lower chambers, or ventricles, which have thick, muscular walls. The wall of the left ventricle is thicker than the right, however. This is because the left *ventricle pumps blood around the body, while the right ventricle only pumps blood the short distance to the lungs. Between each atrium and ventricle is a valve that stops blood flowing backwards as the heart beats. There are also valves in the pulmonary artery, where it leaves the right ventricle, and the aorta, where it leaves the left ventricle.*

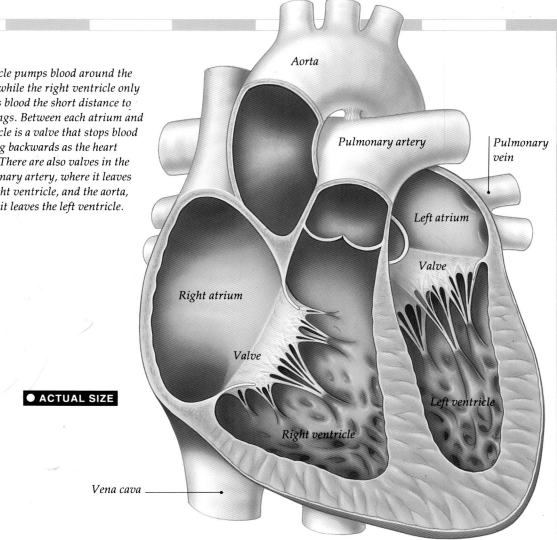

Aorta

Pulmonary artery

Pulmonary vein

Left atrium

Valve

Right atrium

Valve

Left ventricle

Right ventricle

Vena cava

● ACTUAL SIZE

OPEN HEART SURGERY

Open heart surgery involves cutting into the heart or the vessels that supply it with blood. It is made possible by the use of a heart-lung machine. This takes over the job of pumping blood around the body, and adding oxygen to it, until the operation on the heart has finished.

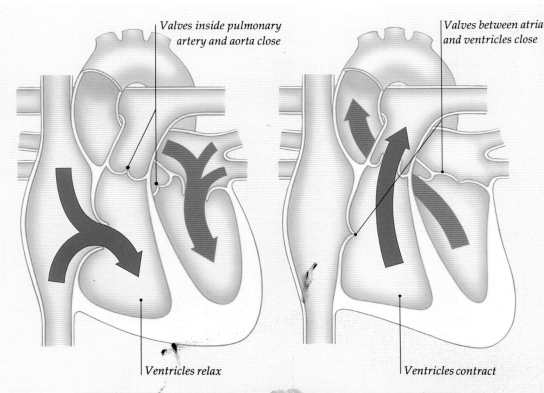

Valves inside pulmonary artery and aorta close

Valves between atria and ventricles close

Ventricles relax

Ventricles contract

PUMPING BLOOD

To imagine how tough and tireless your heart is, clench your fist every second. How long can you keep it up? The muscle in your heart contracts around 100 000 times a day without getting tired. The pumping process takes place in two stages. First, both ventricles

relax. Oxygen-poor blood is drawn into the right ventricle from the body, and oxygen-rich blood into the left ventricle from the lungs. Then both ventricles contract. The valves between atria and ventricles snap shut. Blood is forced from the right ventricle to the lungs, and from the left ventricle to the body.

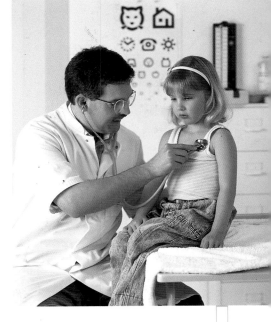

HEART SOUNDS

Doctors can tell a lot about the heart by listening to the sounds it makes with a stethoscope. A healthy heart makes two sounds: 'lub' – which is long and loud – and 'dupp' – which is shorter and softer. Through a stethoscope you would hear: 'lub-dupp', 'lub-dupp'... repeated endlessly. These sounds are produced by the heart valves snapping shut. Unusual heart sounds can tell a doctor that the heart is not pumping properly because its valves are leaking.

Lungs

Every time you breathe, you move air in and out of your lungs. The air you inhale contains around 21 per cent oxygen. Some of this oxygen is absorbed into your bloodstream. The blood carries the oxygen to all body cells. Once inside a cell, oxygen is used to burn food and release the energy locked inside it in a process called respiration. This energy is essential to keep the cell alive and functioning normally. Respiration also releases an unwanted waste product called carbon dioxide, which needs to be disposed of. The blood carries this speedily to the lungs where it is breathed out.

Your two lungs are perfectly adapted to their job. They have a rich blood supply, which makes them pink. They also have millions of tiny channels to carry air, which makes them spongy – so spongy, in fact, that together they weigh just 1 kilogram (2.2 pounds) although they have a total volume of 6 litres (10.5 pints).

OXYGEN SUPPLY
The body's billions of cells demand a non-stop oxygen supply to keep them alive. To satisfy this demand, the heart pumps oxygen-rich blood out to the tissues seventy times a minute - more if you are exercising - in a two-stage process. First, the blood picks up its oxygen supply in the lungs. Then it travels round the body, unloading oxygen as it goes.

WHERE ARE THE LUNGS?
The lungs are found in the chest (thorax), and surround the heart. They are connected to the nasal passage by the windpipe (trachea).

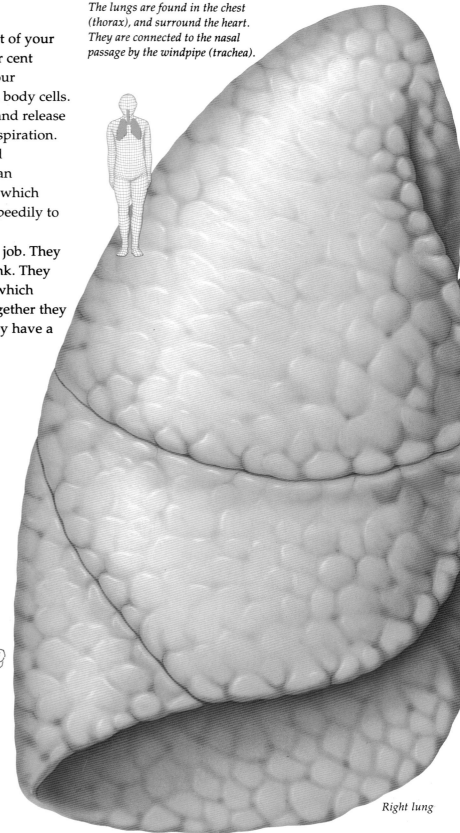

Right lung

Blood carries oxygen to all parts of this athlete's body.

SLIPPERY SURFACES
Lungs are not solid lumps of tissue. They are light and spongy, and filled with millions of air channels which are lined with a thin layer of liquid. The presence of so many air spaces provides an enormous surface for absorbing oxygen from the air you breathe in. In fact, if the lungs could be flattened out they would produce a slippery surface the size of a tennis court.

Windpipe (trachea)

MOUNTAIN AIR
High up in the mountains the air is thinner than at sea level. People who live in places with a high altitude have larger lungs so they can take in more air with each breath and get the right amount of oxygen.

● ACTUAL SIZE

Bronchus

Bronchiole

DAMAGED LUNGS
Cigarette smoke turns healthy pink lung tissue black. Chemicals in cigarette smoke can make lung cells cancerous. These cells multiply out of control, causing lung cancer, which usually kills the smoker.

EXCHANGING GASES
Inside your lungs are 600 million alveoli, which are tiny air bags at the ends of the bronchioles. When you breathe in, oxygen moves from the alveoli into the bloodstream. Carbon dioxide which is not needed by the body, moves from the blood into the alveoli and is breathed out.

Oxygen moves into blood

Carbon dioxide moves out of blood

Alveolus

Bronchiole

Air sac

Left lung

INSIDE THE LUNGS
A look inside the lungs reveals a structure resembling an upside down tree. The 'trunk' of this tree is the windpipe, or trachea. Its main 'branches' are the two bronchi. Each bronchus divides into smaller and smaller branches. The smallest 'twigs' of the tree, the bronchioles, are less than 1 mm wide. At the end of bronchioles are clusters of tiny air bags called alveoli.

Blood capillary

Breathing

You might be able to live without food for weeks, or without water for days, but breathing is something you have to do, without stopping, every day of your life. Breathing moves air in and out of the lungs, bringing oxygen into the body and removing waste carbon dioxide. You can tell this exchange of gases is happening because the air you breathe in contains about 21 per cent oxygen and a tiny amount of carbon dioxide, and the air you breathe out contains less oxygen, about 16 per cent, and more carbon dioxide, up to 4 per cent.

Breathing can be confusing. Most people think your chest is moving because you are breathing. In fact, you are breathing because your chest is moving. The lungs are floppy and passive. They cannot expand on their own. They need the chest to get bigger to expand them and draw air in, and to get smaller to compress them and push the air out again.

THE BREATHING SYSTEM
Air is taken into the breathing system through the nose where it is warmed up and moistened. It travels down the throat, down the windpipe, which is held open by cartilage rings, and into the lungs. The rib cage surrounding the lungs, and the diaphragm below the lungs, cause the chest movements that draw air in and out of the lungs during breathing.

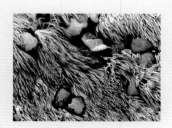

AIR FILTERS
The air you breathe is rarely completely clean, especially in towns and cities. It contains particles of all shapes and sizes, such as dust, grit and pollen grains. If you breathed these in, they could damage the delicate tissues of the lungs. So the air is automatically filtered as you breathe it. Hairs, and sticky mucus, trap particles inside the nose. Mucus also traps particles along the length of the windpipe. As it does so, the mucus is propelled upwards by tiny, hair-like cilia (above) that beat to and fro. When it reaches the throat, it is swallowed.

VENTILATING THE LUNGS
To breathe in, your diaphragm, the muscle at the bottom of the chest, flattens and pushes downwards. At the same time, muscles pull your ribs upwards and outwards. The movements of your diaphragm and ribs expand your chest, sucking air into the lungs from outside. When you breathe out the opposite happens. The diaphragm relaxes and is pushed upwards. The ribs move downwards and inwards. This makes the chest smaller, squeezing air out of the lungs.

BREATHING IN
Ribcage moves upwards and outwards

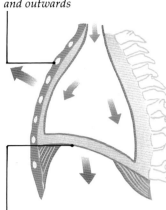

*Diaphragm pushes downwards
As the chest expands,
so do the lungs
Air is sucked into the lungs*

BREATHING OUT
Ribs move downwards and inwards

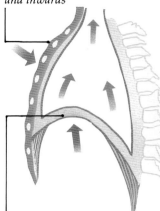

*Diaphragm is pushed upwards
As the chest gets smaller,
so do the lungs
Air is squeezed out of the lungs*

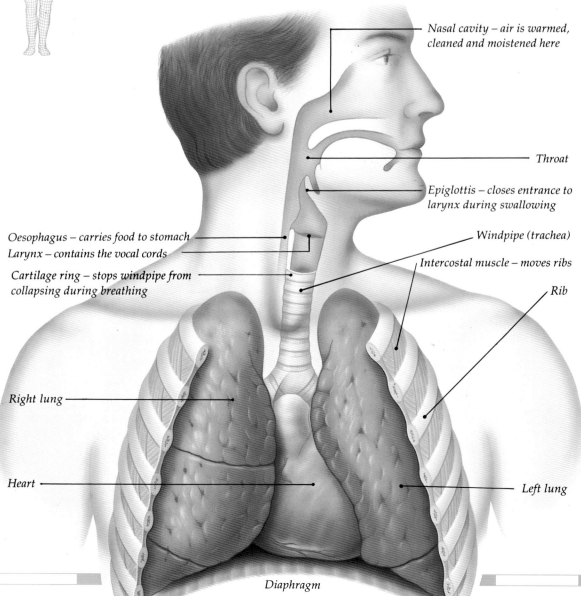

Nasal cavity – air is warmed, cleaned and moistened here

Throat

Epiglottis – closes entrance to larynx during swallowing

Oesophagus – carries food to stomach

Larynx – contains the vocal cords

Cartilage ring – stops windpipe from collapsing during breathing

Windpipe (trachea)

Intercostal muscle – moves ribs

Rib

Right lung

Heart

Left lung

Diaphragm

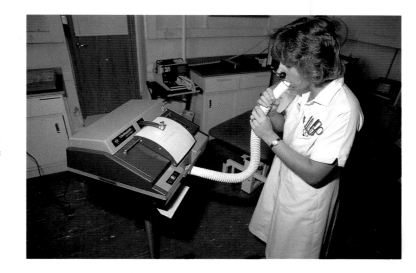

EXERCISING THE LUNGS
Your breathing rate depends on how active you are. At rest you would probably breathe around 15 times each minute. With each breath you would take in about 600 ml (1 pint) of air. When you exercise, your breathing rate, and the amount of air taken in, both go up. A sprinting athlete would breathe about 25 times per second. With each breath, he or she would take in five times as much air as normal to keep up with the body's demand for oxygen. A spirometer (right) measures the volume of air breathed in and out.

MAKING SOUNDS
You make sounds inside your voice box, or larynx. Stretched across the larynx are the vocal cords (below). When these are nearly closed, and air is forced through them, they vibrate, producing sounds. When tight, they produce high-pitched sounds. When loose, they produce low-pitched sounds.

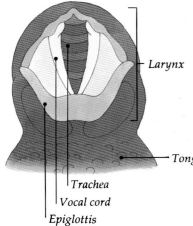

— Larynx

— Tongue

Trachea
Vocal cord
Epiglottis

UNUSUAL MOVEMENTS
Sneezing, hiccuping, laughing and coughing (below) are all unusual breathing movements. Sneezing is a sudden release of built-up air pressure which blows dust from your nose. Coughing is a sudden blast of air that clears any particles from the windpipe. Laughing is caused by sudden contractions of the diaphragm, forcing air out in spurts. Hiccups happen when the diaphragm is irritated. It suddenly flattens and sucks in air.

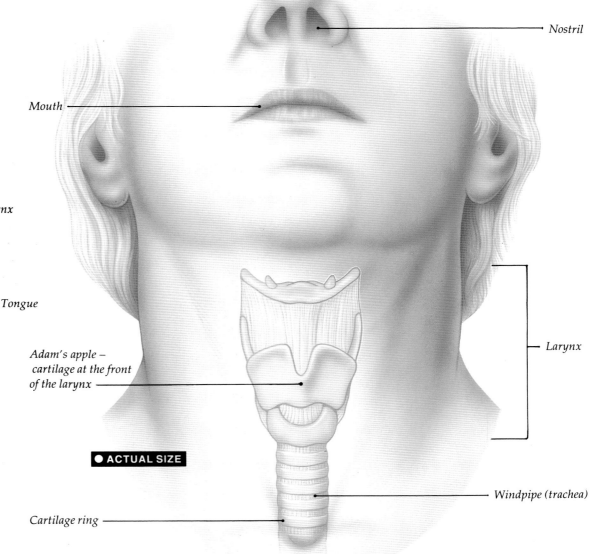

— Nostril

Mouth —

Larynx

Adam's apple – cartilage at the front of the larynx —

● ACTUAL SIZE

— Windpipe (trachea)

Cartilage ring —

Sneezing

Hiccuping

Laughing

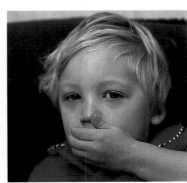

Coughing

Mouth and throat

Food is essential for life. It provides the energy needed for all the body's activities. It enables children to grow into adults. It repairs parts of the body as they wear out. And it provides an insulating layer which keeps you warm. Before food can do any of these jobs, however, it has to be changed into a form the body can use. This task is carried out by the digestive system, essentially a long tube, up to 9 metres (29 feet) long, that runs from mouth to anus. As food passes along the digestive system, it is broken down into smaller and simpler pieces. The food can now be absorbed into the bloodstream and used by the body.

Food enters the digestive system through the mouth and throat. Inside the mouth, food is bitten and crushed in preparation for its journey down the throat.

PROCESSING FOOD

Seeing chewed-up food in someone's mouth is not very pleasant. However, it highlights how food changes between plate and throat. Different parts of the mouth have different roles in this process. Teeth grab food, then chop, tear and grind it into small pieces. The strong, muscular tongue crushes and mixes the food. Salivary glands squirt saliva into the mouth, wetting the food and making it slimy enough to swallow. Lips stop the food from falling out.

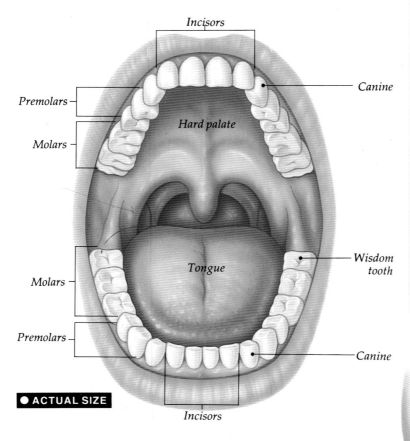

Incisors

Premolars

Molars

Hard palate

Canine

Tongue

Molars

Wisdom tooth

Premolars

Canine

● ACTUAL SIZE

Incisors

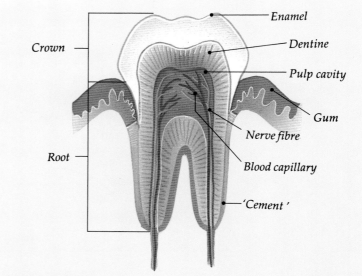

Crown — Enamel

— Dentine

— Pulp cavity

Root

Gum

Nerve fibre

Blood capillary

'Cement'

INSIDE A TOOTH

Teeth are tough. They have to be in order to withstand the years of biting, crushing and grinding. By cutting a tooth in half, you can see where its toughness comes from. Its crown is covered by enamel, the hardest material in the entire body. To stop it falling out, this molar's root is held firmly in its socket by 'cement'.

TYPES OF TEETH

Teeth come in various shapes and sizes. The flat ones at the front are called incisors. They chop food into chunks small enough to fit into your mouth. Next to them are the more pointed canines that grip and tear food when you are biting something tough. Now come the premolars and molars. Broad and flat, they crush and grind food into tiny pieces for swallowing. Do you have the same number of teeth as the picture above?

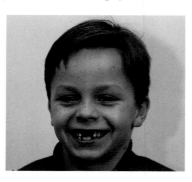

SETS OF TEETH

Babies' first teeth, the milk teeth, appear at six months. By the age of two, a child has a full set of 20. Below them, a second set of permanent teeth is growing. As these erupt from the jaw, the milk teeth fall out. There are 32 permanent teeth – the last four of these, the 'wisdom' teeth, may not arrive until the age of twenty, if at all.

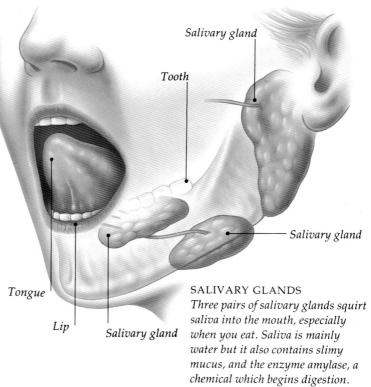

Salivary gland

Tooth

Tongue

Lip

Salivary gland

Salivary gland

SALIVARY GLANDS

Three pairs of salivary glands squirt saliva into the mouth, especially when you eat. Saliva is mainly water but it also contains slimy mucus, and the enzyme amylase, a chemical which begins digestion.

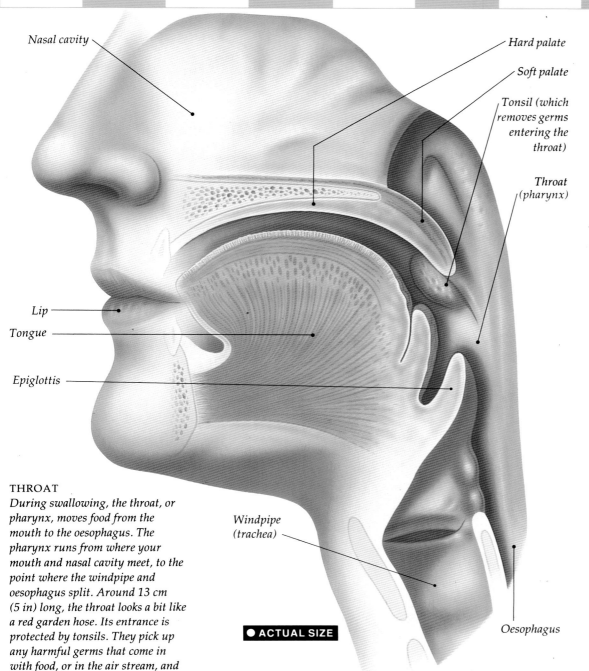

Nasal cavity

Hard palate

Soft palate

Tonsil (which removes germs entering the throat)

Throat (pharynx)

Lip

Tongue

Epiglottis

Windpipe (trachea)

● ACTUAL SIZE

Oesophagus

THROAT

During swallowing, the throat, or pharynx, moves food from the mouth to the oesophagus. The pharynx runs from where your mouth and nasal cavity meet, to the point where the windpipe and oesophagus split. Around 13 cm (5 in) long, the throat looks a bit like a red garden hose. Its entrance is protected by tonsils. They pick up any harmful germs that come in with food, or in the air stream, and destroy them. If you look in a mirror, you can see that your throat is moist and glistening. This is because it produces mucus, which ensures that food slides down it easily.

SWALLOWING

Swallowing sends food on its way along the digestive system. Like the rest of digestion, the process is automatic. Swallowing is made easier because chewed food is coated with slippery mucus.

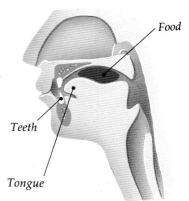

Food

Teeth

Tongue

The tongue pushes food upwards against the hard palate, and backwards into the throat (above). As soon as food touches the throat, a fixed sequence of events begins.

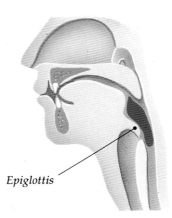

Epiglottis

As throat muscles squeeze food downwards, the lid-like epiglottis closes the entrance to the windpipe. This stops food 'going down the wrong way', into the lungs and choking the eater.

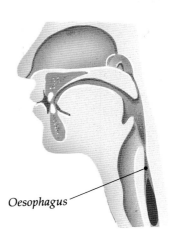

Oesophagus

Once food enters the oesophagus, waves of muscle contractions push it to the stomach. These waves are called peristalsis. From throat to stomach takes around five seconds.

HEALTHY DIET

Your diet, the food you eat every day, must include a mixture of foods to be healthy. This mixture should provide seven nutrients in balanced amounts. Two of these nutrients – proteins and carbohydrates – are needed in quite large amounts. The body needs proteins in order to grow and repair itself. Carbohydrates provide energy, as do fats. Fats, fibre, vitamins and minerals are needed in smaller amounts. Fats also help keep you warm. Fibre is not digested, but it helps the digestive system work properly. Vitamins and minerals ensure body cells work properly. The seventh nutrient is water.

Carbohydrate-rich foods

Protein-rich foods

Fat-rich foods

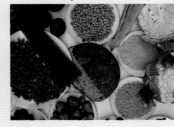

Fibre-rich foods

Stomach and liver

Your stomach and liver are not connected to each other, but sit together in the body. Both of them are involved in digestion.

Your stomach is a part of the long digestive tube running from your mouth to your anus. It is an enlarged area, shaped like a 'J', with muscular walls. Its job is to store food and process it. Empty, your stomach has a volume of about 60 millilitres (0.1 pint), but it can expand to hold over 2 litres (3.5 pints) of food after a big meal. Receptors in the stomach wall detect the wall stretching and tell your brain that you are full. Food generally remains in the stomach for around four hours, although fatty foods stay in the stomach longer. This explains why you feel full longer after eating chips than after eating bread.

Your liver processes recently digested food when it arrives in the blood from the small intestine (see pages 32–33). It also makes a liquid called bile that is squirted back into the small intestine, where it helps digest the fatty food that spent so much time in the stomach. The liver is dark and red because of the large amounts of blood passing through it.

WHERE ARE THE STOMACH AND LIVER?
Both stomach and liver are found in the abdomen, just below the chest. The stomach lies on the left side, nearly hidden by the liver. The liver occupies more space on the right of the abdomen than the left.

STOMACH ENZYMES
Digestion is impossible without enzymes. These chemical digesters turn complex food molecules into simpler ones, which can be absorbed into the blood. The stomach produces two enzymes, pepsin and rennin. Pepsin breaks down proteins into simpler polypeptides. Rennin, produced only in young children, makes milk lumpy, so it stays in the stomach long enough to be digested.

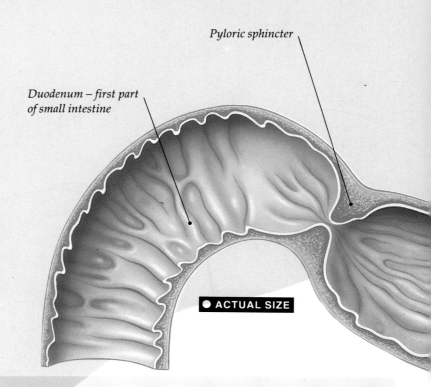

Pyloric sphincter

Duodenum – first part of small intestine

● **ACTUAL SIZE**

HOW THE LIVER WORKS
The liver performs over 500 functions, most of which involve regulating what should be in the blood, and removing what should not be. One major function is to process food arriving from the small intestine, storing some, converting some, and allowing the rest to travel to where it is needed. It removes poisons and drugs from the blood. It makes bile, used to help digest fat in the small intestine. And the heat the liver generates doing all this work helps keep the body warm.

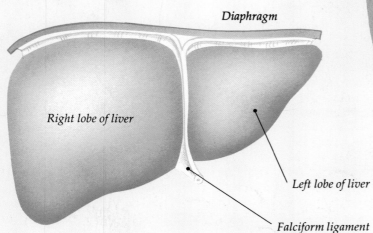

Diaphragm

Right lobe of liver

Left lobe of liver

Falciform ligament

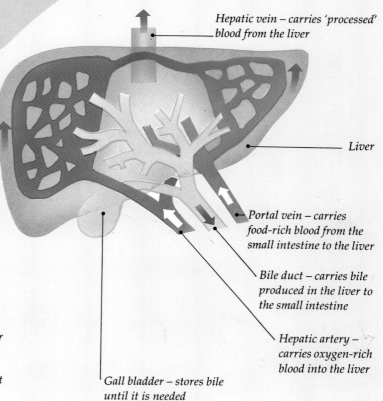

Hepatic vein – carries 'processed' blood from the liver

Liver

Portal vein – carries food-rich blood from the small intestine to the liver

Bile duct – carries bile produced in the liver to the small intestine

Hepatic artery – carries oxygen-rich blood into the liver

Gall bladder – stores bile until it is needed

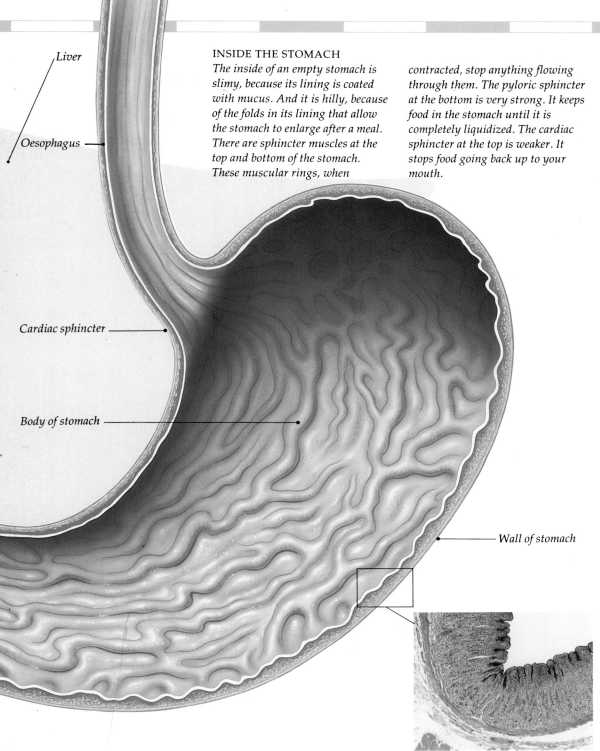

Liver

Oesophagus

Cardiac sphincter

Body of stomach

Wall of stomach

INSIDE THE STOMACH

The inside of an empty stomach is slimy, because its lining is coated with mucus. And it is hilly, because of the folds in its lining that allow the stomach to enlarge after a meal. There are sphincter muscles at the top and bottom of the stomach. These muscular rings, when contracted, stop anything flowing through them. The pyloric sphincter at the bottom is very strong. It keeps food in the stomach until it is completely liquidized. The cardiac sphincter at the top is weaker. It stops food going back up to your mouth.

BEING SICK

Usually you vomit to rid your body of something nasty. The muscles of the abdomen contract, squeezing the stomach's contents up the oesophagus and out of your mouth.

HEARTBURN

This chest pain, due to over-eating, has nothing to do with the heart. It's caused by the stomach acid leaking into the oesophagus and burning its lining.

GASTRIC PITS

Millions of microscopic holes called gastric pits cover the stomach's lining. These pits produce mucus, acid and enzymes. The thick mucus coats the stomach lining and stops it being burnt by the acid. The acid provides the right environment for the enzymes. And the enzymes digest the food.

STOMACH CHURNING

Food arrives in the stomach in the form of chunks. By the time it leaves, some four hours later, it resembles thick, creamy soup. What happens in between?

Well, the stomach is not just a rest area on the journey from mouth to anus. Its wall contains three layers of muscles that run around, along and across the stomach. Their combined action twists, kneads, pummels and crushes the food, and mixes it with digestive gastric juice.

At the same time, the muscles push the food mixture towards the pyloric end of the stomach, the exit point to the small intestine. Here, liquid food is squeezed into the intestine and any lumps are recycled for further crushing.

About five seconds after swallowing, a slimy ball of food, called a bolus, drops into the stomach, which is already starting to expand.

After two hours of kneading and crushing by stomach muscles, and digestion by gastric juice, food has been liquidized into 'creamy soup' that is called chyme.

After four hours, stomach muscles squeeze squirts of chyme through a slightly opened pyloric sphincter. The stomach starts to deflate – unless you have eaten again.

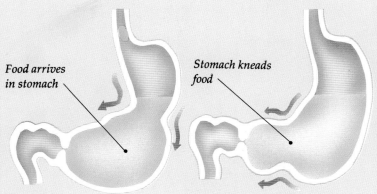

Food arrives in stomach

Stomach kneads food

Chyme squirted through pyloric sphincter

Intestines

The small and large intestines form the last and longest part of the digestive system, where as much goodness as possible is extracted from the food you eat. The intestines are surrounded by layers of smooth muscle which contract slowly and rhythmically, pushing the food along as it is digested and absorbed.

By the time food enters the small intestine from the stomach, it has been in the body for around four hours. As it passes through the small intestine, from duodenum to jejunum to ileum, it is bombarded with digestive chemicals called enzymes which break the food down into smaller and smaller particles. Now they are small enough to slip through the intestinal wall and into the blood transport system, where they are carried around your body. Anything that cannot be digested is squeezed into the large intestine, ready to be removed from the body.

WHERE ARE THE INTESTINES?
The small and large intestines take up most of the space in the abdomen. The abdomen is between the chest and hips.

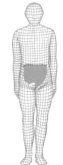

HOW LONG?
Together the small and large intestines are over 6 m (20 ft) long. The small intestine is 5 m (16.4 ft) long and the large intestine is 1.5 m (5 ft) long. To fit into the small space available, they are coiled up around each other.

INSIDE THE INTESTINES?
Food undergoes dramatic changes as it travels along the winding, dark intestinal tunnel. In the small intestine, food is digested chemically, then absorbed. The digestion is done by enzymes, which break down large food particles into small ones. Tiny particles are absorbed through the wall of the small intestine into the blood. The blood carries it to every part of the body, where it can be used to produce energy or growth. Any food that cannot be digested passes on into the large intestine. Here all waste material is dried out before being pushed out through the anus.

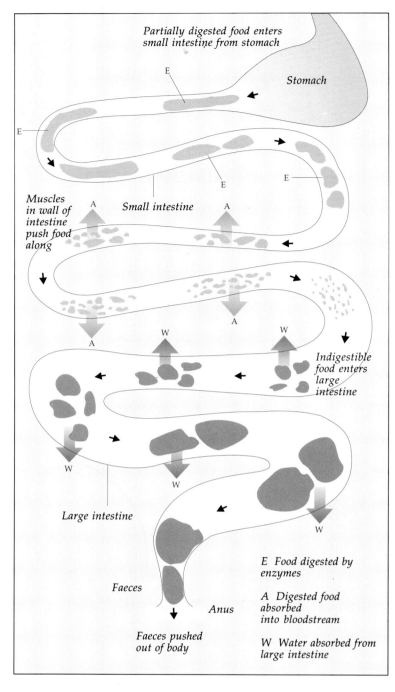

Partially digested food enters small intestine from stomach

E

Stomach

E

E

E

Small intestine

Muscles in wall of intestine push food along

A

A

A

W

W

Indigestible food enters large intestine

Large intestine

W

W

Faeces

Anus

W

Faeces pushed out of body

E Food digested by enzymes

A Digested food absorbed into bloodstream

W Water absorbed from large intestine

5m

HOW WIDE?
If the small intestine is so much longer than the large intestine, why is it called the small intestine? The reason is that the 'large' and 'small' refer to the width rather than the length.

Large intestine

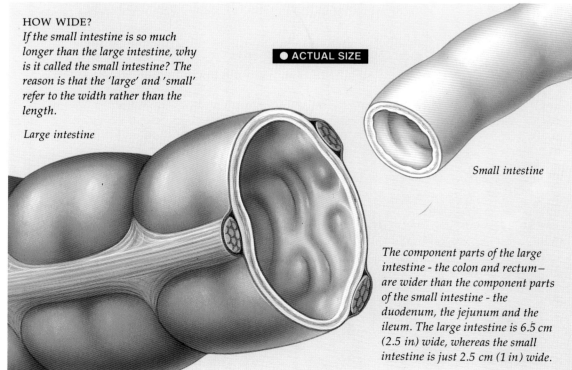

● ACTUAL SIZE

Small intestine

The component parts of the large intestine - the colon and rectum— are wider than the component parts of the small intestine - the duodenum, the jejunum and the ileum. The large intestine is 6.5 cm (2.5 in) wide, whereas the small intestine is just 2.5 cm (1 in) wide.

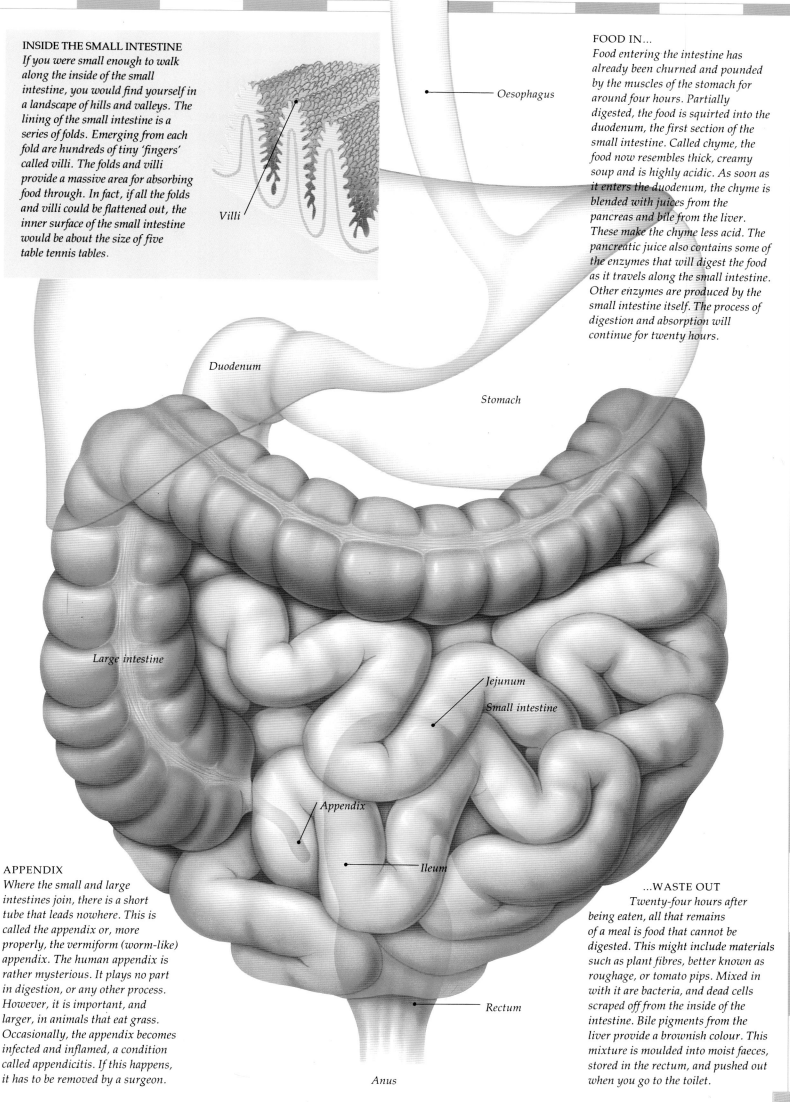

INSIDE THE SMALL INTESTINE
If you were small enough to walk along the inside of the small intestine, you would find yourself in a landscape of hills and valleys. The lining of the small intestine is a series of folds. Emerging from each fold are hundreds of tiny 'fingers' called villi. The folds and villi provide a massive area for absorbing food through. In fact, if all the folds and villi could be flattened out, the inner surface of the small intestine would be about the size of five table tennis tables.

Villi

FOOD IN...
Food entering the intestine has already been churned and pounded by the muscles of the stomach for around four hours. Partially digested, the food is squirted into the duodenum, the first section of the small intestine. Called chyme, the food now resembles thick, creamy soup and is highly acidic. As soon as it enters the duodenum, the chyme is blended with juices from the pancreas and bile from the liver. These make the chyme less acid. The pancreatic juice also contains some of the enzymes that will digest the food as it travels along the small intestine. Other enzymes are produced by the small intestine itself. The process of digestion and absorption will continue for twenty hours.

Oesophagus

Duodenum

Stomach

Large intestine

Jejunum

Small intestine

Appendix

Ileum

APPENDIX
Where the small and large intestines join, there is a short tube that leads nowhere. This is called the appendix or, more properly, the vermiform (worm-like) appendix. The human appendix is rather mysterious. It plays no part in digestion, or any other process. However, it is important, and larger, in animals that eat grass. Occasionally, the appendix becomes infected and inflamed, a condition called appendicitis. If this happens, it has to be removed by a surgeon.

...WASTE OUT
Twenty-four hours after being eaten, all that remains of a meal is food that cannot be digested. This might include materials such as plant fibres, better known as roughage, or tomato pips. Mixed in with it are bacteria, and dead cells scraped off from the inside of the intestine. Bile pigments from the liver provide a brownish colour. This mixture is moulded into moist faeces, stored in the rectum, and pushed out when you go to the toilet.

Rectum

Anus

Waste disposal

Several times a day, you stop whatever you are doing to urinate. The urine you pass out of your body is the product of a process of waste disposal carried out by your urinary system.

Wastes are produced by the chemical processes taking place inside all the body's cells. If they were allowed to build up, these wastes would poison you. Instead, they are filtered out of the blood as it travels through the kidneys. But the kidneys do more than simply remove wastes. They control the amount of water and salts inside the body. If you drink lots of water, or eat salty food, the kidneys will remove the excess.

Urine consists of filtered wastes, along with excess water and salts. 180 litres (40 gallons) of liquid is filtered out of the 1 700 litres (374 gallons) of blood that flow through the kidneys each day. Most is absorbed back into the body, otherwise you would rapidly shrivel up due to water loss. Only 1.5 litres (2.5 pints) a day is discharged as urine. This trickles down the ureters into the bladder. And when the bladder is full, it sends a message to your brain.

WHERE ARE THE KIDNEYS?
Your urinary system runs from the kidneys, which lie behind the liver and stomach, down the ureters to the bladder and out through the urethra.

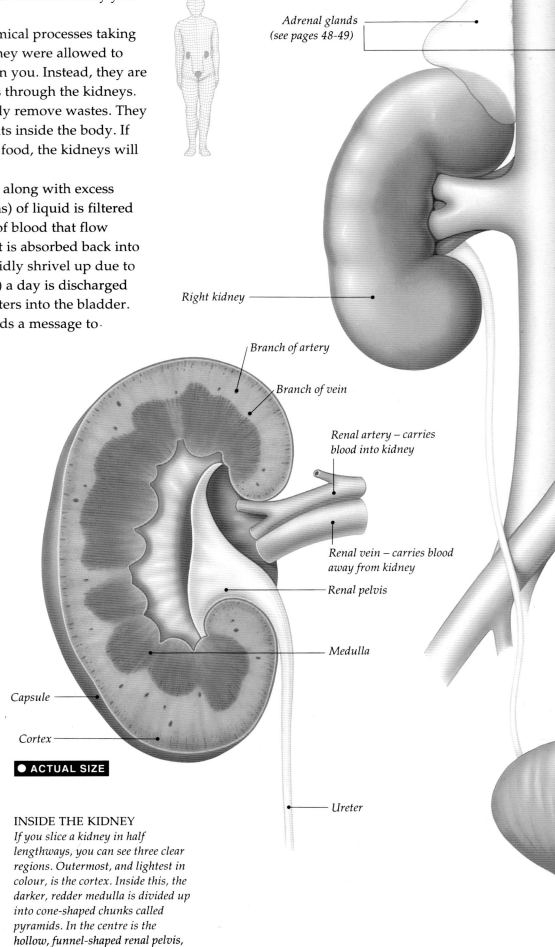

Adrenal glands
(see pages 48-49)

Right kidney

Branch of artery

Branch of vein

Renal artery – carries blood into kidney

Renal vein – carries blood away from kidney

Renal pelvis

Medulla

Capsule

Cortex

● ACTUAL SIZE

Ureter

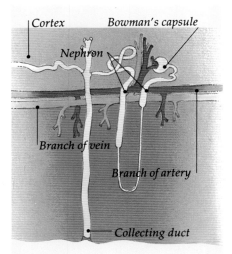

Cortex

Bowman's capsule

Nephron

Branch of vein

Branch of artery

Collecting duct

FILTRATION UNITS
Blood is cleaned in millions of tiny filtration units called nephrons, which travel in twists and turns between cortex and medulla. Liquid is forced out of the blood as it passes through the knot of capillaries inside the hollow, cup-shaped Bowman's capsule. This filtered liquid contains not only water and waste, but also useful substances, such as glucose, which the body cannot afford to lose. As the liquid moves along the coiled nephron, most water and all the useful substances are taken back into the bloodstream. What remains – a mixture of water and waste – is called urine. Concentrated in the collecting duct, the urine drains into the renal pelvis and ureter.

INSIDE THE KIDNEY
If you slice a kidney in half lengthways, you can see three clear regions. Outermost, and lightest in colour, is the cortex. Inside this, the darker, redder medulla is divided up into cone-shaped chunks called pyramids. In the centre is the hollow, funnel-shaped renal pelvis, which runs into the ureter.

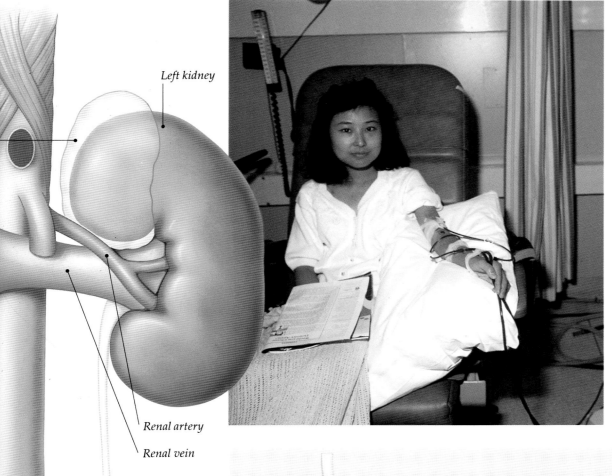

Left kidney

Renal artery

Renal vein

Ureter

Bladder

ARTIFICIAL KIDNEY

What happens if kidneys stop working? Well, if one kidney fails, the other takes over its job. But if both kidneys fail, poisonous wastes build up in the bloodstream, threatening the person's life. In the past, they would have died. Now, by using an artificial kidney, they have a chance.

Inside an artificial kidney is a mass of tubing made out of a material similar to cellophane. Surrounding the tubing is a liquid called dialysis fluid. The patient is linked to the artificial kidney by a tube connected to one of his or her arteries. As blood is pumped through the mass of tubing, wastes pass out of it and into the dialysis fluid. The purified blood then passes along another tube, and back into the patient through a vein. To avoid becoming ill, the patient must use the artificial kidney for around six hours, three times a week.

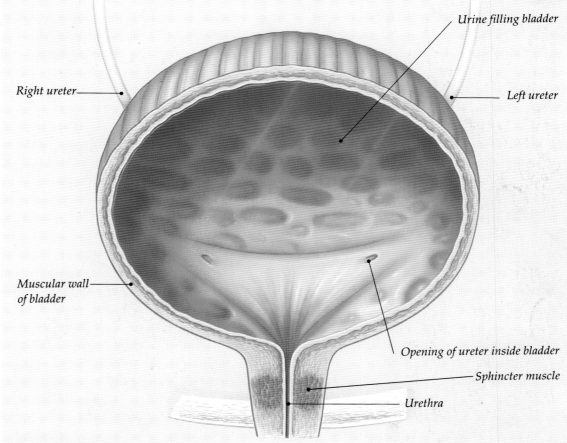

Right ureter

Urine filling bladder

Left ureter

Muscular wall of bladder

Opening of ureter inside bladder

Sphincter muscle

Urethra

HOW THE BLADDER WORKS

Your bladder is an elastic, muscular bag. It stores the urine that is made continuously in the kidneys. Urine is squirted into the bladder through the openings of the two ureters. The exit, through the urethra, is clamped shut by a ring of muscle called a sphincter.

The bladder is the size of a walnut when it is empty. It expands like a balloon as it fills with urine. When it contains about 150 ml (0.25 pints) of urine,

receptors in the bladder wall detect the surface stretching and send a message to the brain. Then you feel the need to go to the toilet. However, the bladder can continue to fill until it contains over 600 ml (1 pint) – two soft drink cans full – of urine. By this time you are desperate to go. Then when you relax the sphincter muscle, the muscles in the bladder wall push inwards, and the urine flows out.

Brain

Touch the side of your head. Just two centimetres from your fingertips, floating in a shockproofing fluid, and protected by the bony skull, lies 1.5 kilograms (3 pounds) of soft, pink-grey tissue, wrinkled on the outside like a walnut. This is your brain.

Your brain is your body's control centre. It enables you to think, touch, hear, see, smell and taste. It stores your memories, emotions and feelings. It lets you learn, understand and have ideas. It co-ordinates and regulates all body functions, even when you sleep.

Look inside and all you will see is a mass of nerve cells. Although the brain makes up just 2 per cent of the body's weight, these cells consume about 25 per cent of the body's energy. Working together, they enable you to recognize over 10 000 faces. In fact, your brain has immense powers above and beyond any computer yet built.

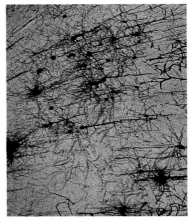

HOW MANY CELLS?
You have over 10 thousand million nerve cells in your brain. This is an unimaginably large number, more than the number of stars in the Andromeda galaxy (above).

COMMUNICATION NETWORK
Between your 10 thousand million brain cells there are over 10 million million connections. This network is not fixed, though. New connections are made all the time.

WHERE IS THE BRAIN?
Your brain is wrapped in three layers of membranes, and encased within the bony cranium. Here it floats in a sea of fluid, which protects it against accidental knocks.

Your motor area sends instructions to your muscles, enabling you to move and balance. It also controls learned skills such as playing sports or a musical instrument.

Your sensory area receives information from skin sensors all over the body. This is where you 'feel' the outside world.

HOW THE BRAIN WORKS
The control centre of your brain is the cerebral cortex. Some areas of the cortex receive and sort incoming messages from certain parts of the body. Others send out instructions.

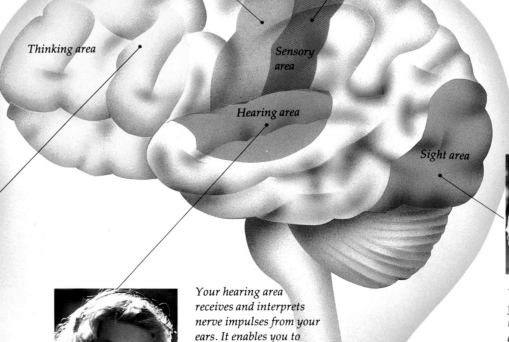

Motor area

Thinking area

Sensory area

Hearing area

Sight area

The area at the front of your brain is the most complex part. It enables you to think, learn, plan and have feelings and emotions. This is the home of your personality.

Your hearing area receives and interprets nerve impulses from your ears. It enables you to distinguish music from noise, thunder from a human voice.

Your sight area is where you see. Nerve impulses that travel from the eye along the optic nerve are turned into pictures here.

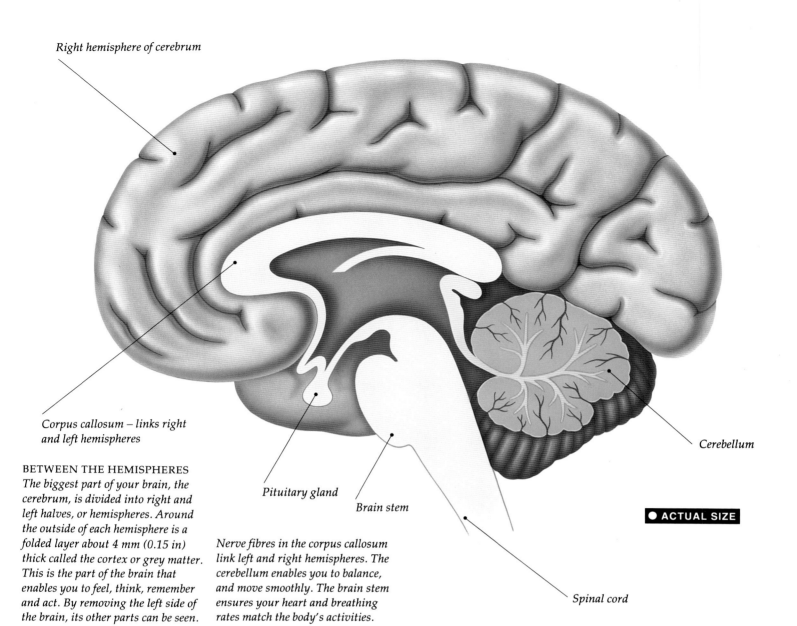

Right hemisphere of cerebrum

Corpus callosum – links right and left hemispheres

Pituitary gland

Brain stem

Cerebellum

Spinal cord

● ACTUAL SIZE

BETWEEN THE HEMISPHERES
The biggest part of your brain, the cerebrum, is divided into right and left halves, or hemispheres. Around the outside of each hemisphere is a folded layer about 4 mm (0.15 in) thick called the cortex or grey matter. This is the part of the brain that enables you to feel, think, remember and act. By removing the left side of the brain, its other parts can be seen.

Nerve fibres in the corpus callosum link left and right hemispheres. The cerebellum enables you to balance, and move smoothly. The brain stem ensures your heart and breathing rates match the body's activities.

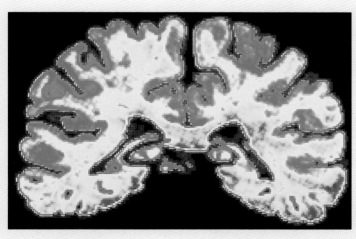

BRAIN SCANS
How can you look inside a brain to see what is wrong with it? In the past, the only way was to cut it open after its owner had died! Now doctors can look inside by using brain scans.

Brain tissue does not show up well on X-rays. But when they are linked to a computer in a CAT or Computerized Axial Tomography scan, the image of a thin 'slice' through the patient's brain, or a 3-D image, can be built up.

Doctors also use Positron Emission Tomography (PET) to examine the brain. A PET scan detects brain activity and shows which part of the brain is working at the time.

LEFT AND RIGHT BRAIN
Each side of your brain controls the actions of the opposite side of your body. Twiddle your left toe, and the instruction comes from the right side of the brain. Each side is also involved with different skills. The right side of the brain deals with art and music; the left side of the brain deals with numbers, words and problem solving.

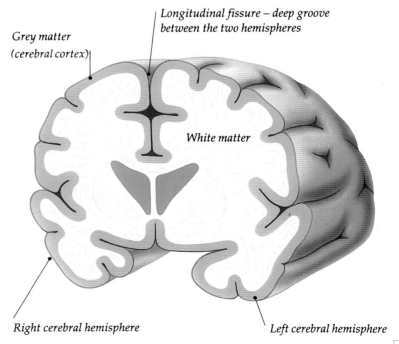

Grey matter (cerebral cortex)

Longitudinal fissure – deep groove between the two hemispheres

White matter

Right cerebral hemisphere

Left cerebral hemisphere

Spinal cord and nerves

It is the nervous system that directly controls the body. At its core are the brain and the spinal cord, which together form the central nervous system (CNS). The brain is the control centre (see pages 36-37), while the spinal cord links the brain with the rest of the body and processes reflex actions. Of course, the CNS cannot control the rest of the body unless it is connected to it. This link is provided by the nerves, which carry information in the form of electrical impulses between the muscles and the sensory organs and the CNS.

Right now, nerves are carrying impulses from your eyes to your brain at a speed of 400 kilometres per hour (248 miles per hour). While your brain interprets the words in front of you, it sends out impulses to the eye muscles, instructing them to move the eyes so you can read the rest of the line. And these are just a few of the three million nerve impulses speeding along the 75-kilometre (47-mile) network of nerves each second.

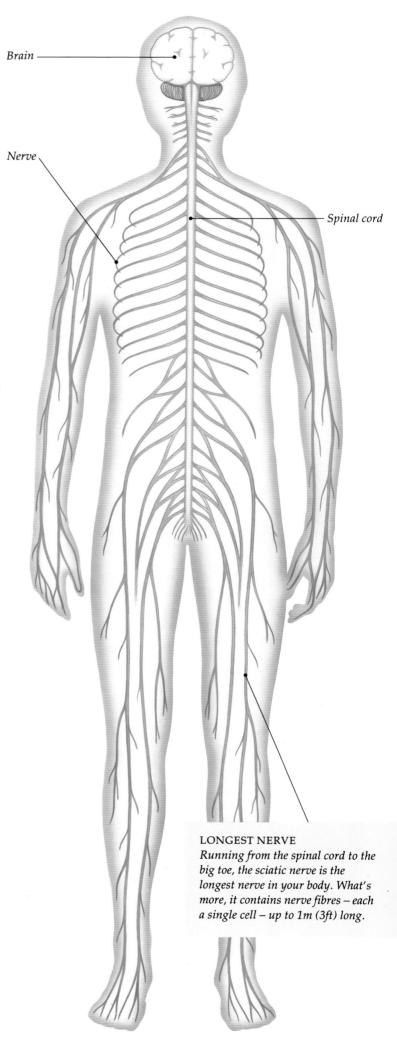

Brain

Nerve

Spinal cord

THE NERVOUS SYSTEM
The brain, the spinal cord and the nerves that connect them to the rest of the body make up the nervous system. In it, each nerve cell (above) communicates with many others to form a massive control network.

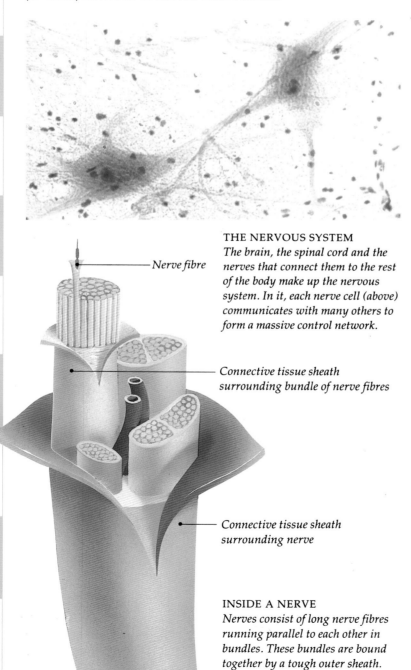

Nerve fibre

Connective tissue sheath
surrounding bundle of nerve fibres

Connective tissue sheath
surrounding nerve

INSIDE A NERVE
Nerves consist of long nerve fibres running parallel to each other in bundles. These bundles are bound together by a tough outer sheath.

LONGEST NERVE
Running from the spinal cord to the big toe, the sciatic nerve is the longest nerve in your body. What's more, it contains nerve fibres – each a single cell – up to 1m (3ft) long.

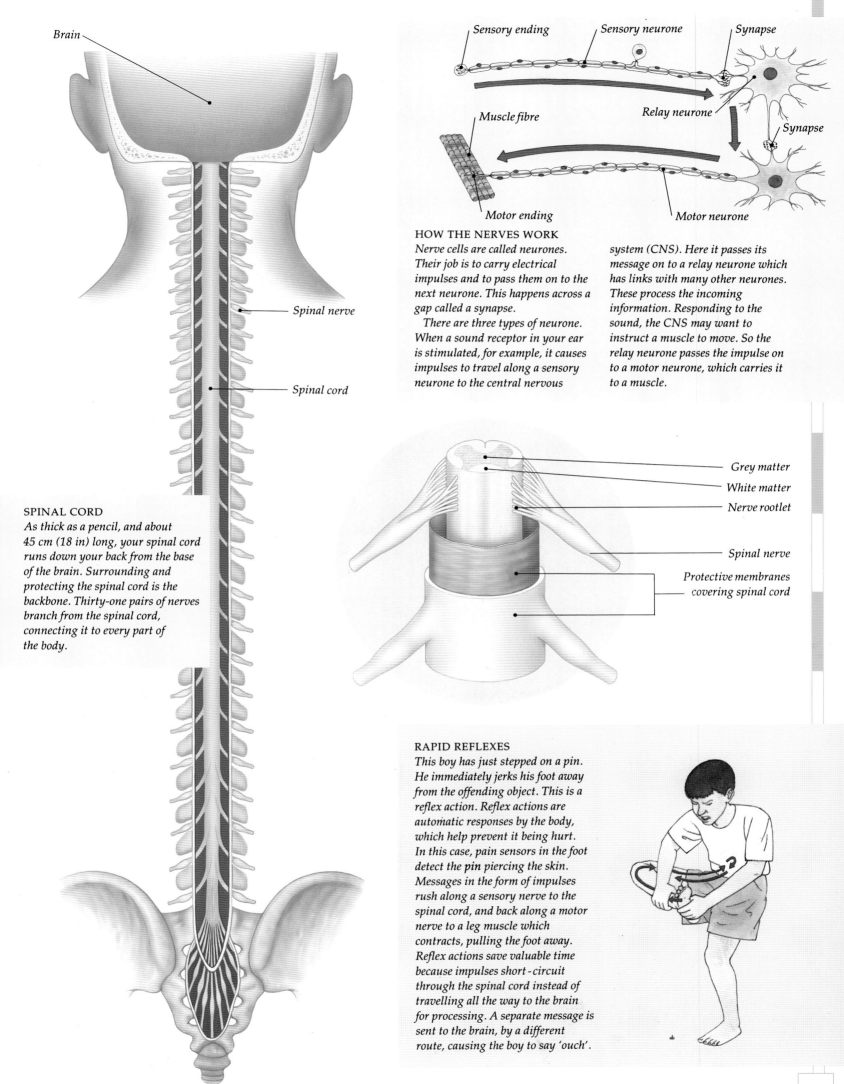

Brain

Spinal nerve

Spinal cord

Sensory ending

Sensory neurone

Synapse

Relay neurone

Synapse

Muscle fibre

Motor ending

Motor neurone

HOW THE NERVES WORK

Nerve cells are called neurones. Their job is to carry electrical impulses and to pass them on to the next neurone. This happens across a gap called a synapse.

There are three types of neurone. When a sound receptor in your ear is stimulated, for example, it causes impulses to travel along a sensory neurone to the central nervous system (CNS). Here it passes its message on to a relay neurone which has links with many other neurones. These process the incoming information. Responding to the sound, the CNS may want to instruct a muscle to move. So the relay neurone passes the impulse on to a motor neurone, which carries it to a muscle.

SPINAL CORD

As thick as a pencil, and about 45 cm (18 in) long, your spinal cord runs down your back from the base of the brain. Surrounding and protecting the spinal cord is the backbone. Thirty-one pairs of nerves branch from the spinal cord, connecting it to every part of the body.

Grey matter

White matter

Nerve rootlet

Spinal nerve

Protective membranes covering spinal cord

RAPID REFLEXES

This boy has just stepped on a pin. He immediately jerks his foot away from the offending object. This is a reflex action. Reflex actions are automatic responses by the body, which help prevent it being hurt. In this case, pain sensors in the foot detect the pin piercing the skin. Messages in the form of impulses rush along a sensory nerve to the spinal cord, and back along a motor nerve to a leg muscle which contracts, pulling the foot away. Reflex actions save valuable time because impulses short-circuit through the spinal cord instead of travelling all the way to the brain for processing. A separate message is sent to the brain, by a different route, causing the boy to say 'ouch'.

Skin

Your skin is a layer just 2 millimetres (0.07 inches) thick which, spread out, would cover an area of 2 square metres (2.4 square yards) – or thirteen times the area of the open book in front of you.

Skin is made of two layers. The outer epidermis replaces the dead cells that are constantly worn away from its surface. It also produces dark melanin that gives skin its colour and protects skin cells from the harmful effects of the sun's ultraviolet rays. The inner dermis contains nerve endings that make the skin sensitive to heat, cold, pain, pressure and touch. It also contains hair follicles that produce hairs, and sebaceous glands, which make the oil that keeps the skin supple.

Skin forms a barrier against germ invasion. It stops water soaking into, or leaking out of the body. It helps you regulate body temperature. Skin is much more than a simple body covering!

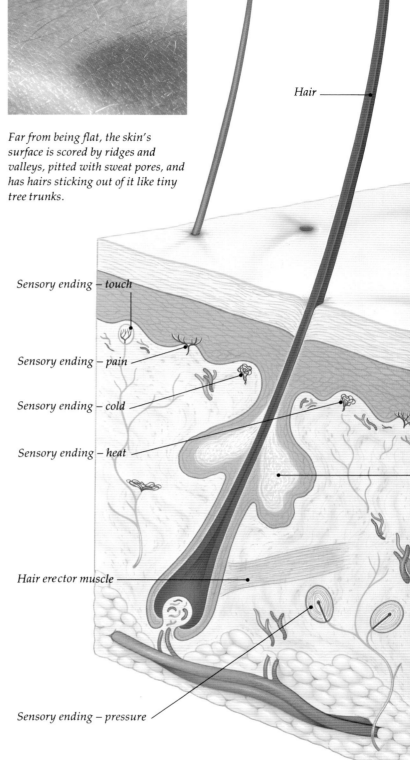

Far from being flat, the skin's surface is scored by ridges and valleys, pitted with sweat pores, and has hairs sticking out of it like tiny tree trunks.

Hair

Sensory ending – touch

Sensory ending – pain

Sensory ending – cold

Sensory ending – heat

Hair erector muscle

Sensory ending – pressure

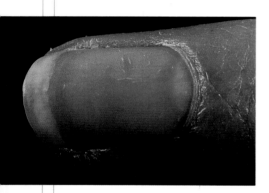

NAILS
Why doesn't it hurt when you cut your nails? Because, although they grow from living cells in the nail root, nails are dead. Like hair, nails are made of tough keratin. They protect the top surface of your fingertips and help you pick up objects. Fingernails grow about 0.5 mm (0.02 in) each week. They grow faster in warm weather and on the hand you use most.

FINGERPRINTS
Look at your fingertips. Each one has its own pattern of ridges which helps you grip objects, just as tyre treads help a car grip a wet road. A thin layer of sticky sweat covers the fingertips, so that if you touch a hard surface, you leave behind a fingerprint – a sweaty copy of the ridge pattern. The whorls and loops of a person's fingerprints are unique and easily identifiable. This is why they are so useful to the police. If they find clear fingerprints at the scene of a crime that match those of a criminal whose records they hold, they can be sure who made them. Sweat pores in fingers may leave 'poreprints' on a surface too.

SKIN SENSITIVITY
The warmth of the summer sun. The shock of diving into an icy pond. The pain of a pinprick. The pressure felt when you shake hands. The soft texture of velvet. You experience all these sensations through your skin. Just below its surface are sensors that detect heat, cold, pain, pressure, and touch. They are not spread evenly over the body, however. Fingertips have more sensors than elbows, for example and feet more than knees. Hands and feet need to be specially sensitive because they are often our first point of contact with objects that may cut or burn.

HEAT SENSORS
You can 'confuse' the heat sensors in your fingertips. Dip one finger in hot water and the other in cold, then dip both together in warm water. The 'hot' finger will feel cold and the 'cold' finger will feel hot.

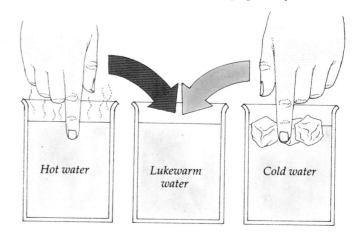

Hot water | Lukewarm water | Cold water

Your hairs are made of dead cells, reinforced with tough keratin, the material found in nails. Hairs are made by follicles. They spring from cells found at the bottom of deep holes in the skin.

HAIR TYPES

There are millions of hairs covering most of the body, apart from the lips, palms of the hands and soles of the feet. These millions of hairs are divided into two main types: the fine hair that covers the bodies of women and children; and the longer, coarser hair found on everybody's head, and on the face and chest of men.

However, when people talk about hair, they usually mean the 100 000 or so hairs on the top of their head. Generally, these are either wavy, straight or curly. The different types depend on the shape of the shaft of the hair. Wavy hair has an oval shaft. Straight hair has a round shaft. And curly hair has a flat shaft that looks like a ribbon.

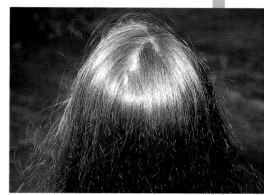

Straight hair

Sweat pore — Epidermis

— Dermis

Sweat duct

...ceous gland

Hair follicle

— Fat layer

— Blood capillary

— Nerve

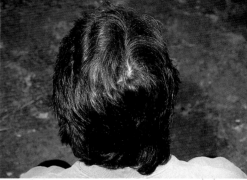

Wavy hair

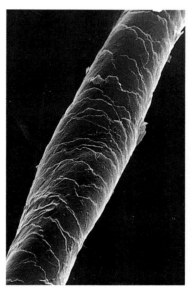

Human hair greatly magnified

Curly hair

SWEAT GLANDS

There are over 3 million sweat glands in your skin. Put end to end they would stretch over 9.5 km (6 miles). Each has a coiled-up part in the dermis that produces sweat, and a tube that carries sweat up to the skin's surface.

Sweat is mainly water with a dash of salt and waste. Usually you release about half a soft drink can-full each day, but this can increase to 1 litre (1.8 pints) a day in hot weather or if you take exercise. Sweat helps you keep cool (see right).

Cooling the body.

Heating the body.

TEMPERATURE CONTROL

Your body manages to keep its temperature remarkably constant – around 37°C (98.6°F) – whatever conditions are like outside. Temperature control is vitally important. If your body gets too hot, or too cold, it will not work properly and you may die.

Skin plays an important part in temperature control. If you are too hot, the blood vessels in the skin get wider and you look flushed. But because more blood is flowing, more heat is lost across the skin. The skin acts like a radiator, cooling the body. At the same time, the sweat glands release lots of extra sweat on to the skin's surface. This evaporates, also cooling the body.

If you are too cold, blood vessels near the skin's surface get narrower. Your muscles contract, making you shiver, releasing heat at the same time. Tiny muscles in the skin also pull on the body's hairs, giving you goose-pimples.

Eyes

From the moment you are born, you depend on your eyes to provide you with a stream of information about shape, colour and movement in the world around you. Most important of the sense organs, the eyes contain 70 per cent of your body's sensory receptors. A million nerve fibres carry information from these receptors to the brain.

The eyeball is just 2.5 centimetres (1 inch) in diameter. Although a tough sclera – the white of the eye – covers most of it, the clear cornea at the front allows light in. This light is focused on the retina on the back of the eye, producing an upside-down image no bigger than a postage stamp. When the light hits the retina's sensory cells, they fire off messages, which are sent along the optic nerve to the brain. Here, in the visual area at the back of the brain, is where you actually see. In a tiny fraction of a second, the coded messages are unscrambled. The visual area of the brain also uses information from the muscles that move the eyes, along with visual clues from the outside, to enable you to judge distances accurately.

COLOUR BLINDNESS
If you cannot see a number in this picture, you are one of the many males, and few females, who are colour-blind. One of the three types of cone (see below) – which recognize red, green or blue – is missing from your retina, so you cannot distinguish certain colours.

WHERE ARE THE EYES?
Your two eyes are located in the front of the upper part of the head facing forwards. Just one-sixth of each eyeball is visible. The rest is cushioned by a pad of fat, inside a protective bony orbit.

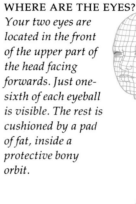

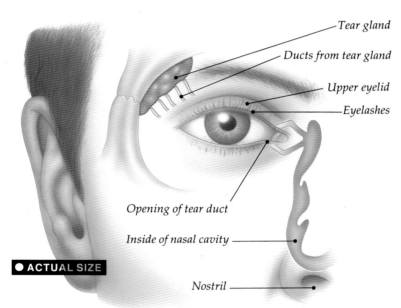

Tear gland

Ducts from tear gland

Upper eyelid

Eyelashes

Opening of tear duct

Inside of nasal cavity

● ACTUAL SIZE

Nostril

Upside-down image of the kite projected onto retina

Retina – light-sensitive layer

Fovea – dip in the retina where cones are concentrated

Blind spot – where optic nerve leaves eye

TEARS AND BLINKING
Generally, you only notice tears when you cry. In fact, you produce tears all the time. Tears form an essential part of the defence system that protects the front of the eye from dirt, dust, smoke and germs carried in the air. They are made in the tear glands just above the eye, then they spread over the front of the eye and moisten it. (Dry eyes feel very uncomfortable.) Tears also contain a chemical called lysozyme that kills germs.

Blinking helps spread tears over the eye. It is a reflex action and happens without you thinking about it, every three to seven seconds. The eyelids sweep tears and dirt into tiny holes in the corner of the eye. These empty into the tear duct which is connected to the nose – which explains why you have to blow your nose when you cry. The blinking reflex also springs into action if something – an insect, say – suddenly approaches the eye, or if something touches the eyelashes, even a puff of air.

RODS AND CONES
In the retina, there are rod and cone cells that are sensitive to light. Your eye's 125 million skinny rods 'see' in black and white only and work best in dim light. The 7 million dumpy cones 'see' in colour and work best in bright light. So in dim light you lose colour vision.

Superior oblique – turns eye downwards and inwards

Superior rectus – rolls eye upwards

Bone of skull

Eyeball

Lateral rectus – turns eye outwards

Optic nerve

Inferior oblique – turns eye upwards and inwards

Inferior rectus – rolls eye downwards

Bone of skull

● ACTUAL SIZE

Eyeball

Lateral rectus – turns eye outwards

Superior rectus – rolls eye upwards

Medial rectus – turns eye inwards

Superior oblique – turns eye downwards and inwards

Trochlea (pulley)

Sclera – white of eye

Choroid – dark layer

MOVING THE EYES

Six strap-like muscles hold each eyeball in place in its socket and pull the eyeball in different directions. The muscle movements are co-ordinated so that your eyes do not swivel in different directions.

When following a moving object, your eyes make slow, scanning movements. When you stare at something, your eyes do not stay still – short, darting movements cover everything in view. Look at something close to you and your eyes swivel inwards. Look at something far away and your eyes point straight ahead.

Conjunctiva – thin, protective layer

Ciliary muscle – changes the shape of the lens

Suspensory ligament – holds the lens in place

FOCUSING

Life would be difficult if all you could see were fuzzy shapes and colours. Fortunately, the cornea focuses light entering the eye on the retina. Fine focusing is done by the lens. The ciliary muscle changes the shape of the lens – fat for near objects, thin for distant objects – so it can focus light from any distance and always produce a sharp image.

Cornea – transparent layer, helps in focusing

Aqueous humour – watery liquid

Pupil – hole where light enters

Lens – helps to focus light on retina

Iris – coloured part of the eye, controls the amount of light entering

Image of kite as seen by the eye

THE IRIS

Look at your eyes in a mirror. In the centre of the coloured part, the iris, you will see a round, black pupil. In fact the pupil is a hole, the entrance to the inner darkness of the eyeball. The iris controls the amount of light entering the eye. In dim light, the iris retracts and your pupils get bigger, allowing more light in. In bright light, the iris expands, the pupils get smaller, stopping too much light getting in and damaging the sensory cells inside.

Bright light

Vitreous humour – jelly-like substance

Dim light

Ears

Sound is produced by a jumbo jet taking off, a crying baby, a classical sonata played on the piano, a whispered comment and a breeze blowing through the leaves of a tree. Your ears enable you to hear all these sounds, whether they are soft or loud, pleasant or unpleasant, high-pitched or low-pitched. They allow you to appreciate the difference between a musical sound and raw noise, and between the voice of a stranger and the voice of a friend.

What most people familiarly call ears – the flaps that stick out from the side of the head – are in fact only a small part of the ear. They direct sound down a small tunnel, or canal, in the side of your head. The ear's inner workings are 4 centimetres (1.5 inches) down that canal.

In the fluid-filled inner ear is the cochlea. This is shaped like a snail shell. Inside it are 20 000 sensory cells, each carrying 100 'hairs'. When these 'hairs' are bent by sounds transmitted through the ear, their sensory cells send nerve impulses to the brain. There, after the impulses are sorted out, you actually hear the sounds.

However, ears are more than just sound-detectors. Part of the inner region of the ear helps you balance by detecting the position of the head, and following its movements.

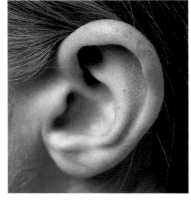

WHERE ARE THE EARS?
Your two ears are located on opposite sides of the head, just below the level of the eye. The ear canal secretes yellow-brown ear wax (cerumen), which traps dust and insects. The ear is self-cleaning. The wax dries up and falls out of the ear. It is constantly being replaced.

CATCHING SOUNDS
Sound waves are channelled into your ear by the shell-shaped pinna that surrounds the opening to the ear canal. Animals can move their ears to pin-point sounds. You have to move your head to do that.

SOUND DETECTION
Sounds travel through the air towards you in the form of waves, rather like the ripples produced when you toss a pebble into a pond. When sound waves travelling down the ear canal hit the eardrum, they make it vibrate. Fixed to the inside of the eardrum are the body's tiniest bones – the hammer, anvil and stirrup, which are named for their shapes. As the eardrum vibrates, it moves the hammer. This causes the anvil to vibrate and push the

stirrup. In turn, the stirrup is connected to the oval window, a membrane-covered hole guarding the entrance to the inner ear. As the stirrup moves in and out like a piston, it sets up vibrations in the fluid inside the cochlea. These vibrations bend tiny 'hairs' on the end of sensory cells, causing them to send nerve impulses along the auditory nerve to the brain. Here the sounds are sorted out so that you hear them.

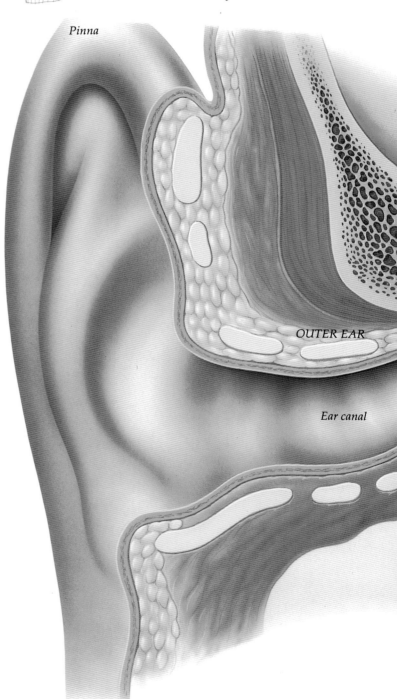

Pinna

OUTER EAR

Ear canal

AIR PRESSURE
The Eustachian tube runs between the middle ear and the throat. It keeps air pressures equal on either side of the eardrum by allowing the eardrum to vibrate properly. By

yawning or swallowing, you open the entrance to the tube. If air pressure changes suddenly, as it does when a plane takes off, swallowing helps you hear normally again.

● **ACTUAL SIZE**

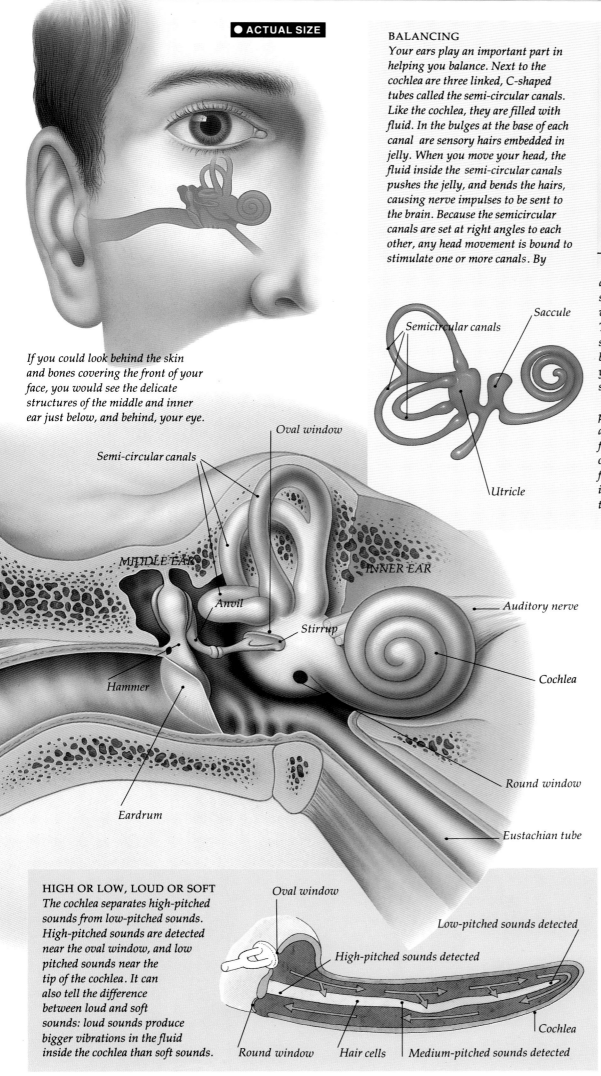

If you could look behind the skin and bones covering the front of your face, you would see the delicate structures of the middle and inner ear just below, and behind, your eye.

Semi-circular canals

Oval window

MIDDLE EAR

INNER EAR

Anvil

Stirrup

Auditory nerve

Hammer

Cochlea

Eardrum

Round window

Eustachian tube

BALANCING

Your ears play an important part in helping you balance. Next to the cochlea are three linked, C-shaped tubes called the semi-circular canals. Like the cochlea, they are filled with fluid. In the bulges at the base of each canal are sensory hairs embedded in jelly. When you move your head, the fluid inside the semi-circular canals pushes the jelly, and bends the hairs, causing nerve impulses to be sent to the brain. Because the semicircular canals are set at right angles to each other, any head movement is bound to stimulate one or more canals. By

Semicircular canals

Saccule

Utricle

detecting which canals have been stimulated, the brain works out which way the head is moving. The utricle and saccule, next to the semicircular canals, also help you balance. They tell the brain whether you are upright, lying down, or standing on your head.

Other parts of the body also play a part in balance. Your brain receives a constant stream of information from pressure receptors in the soles of your feet, from your eyes and from your muscles and joints to help it produce an up-to-date picture of the position you are in.

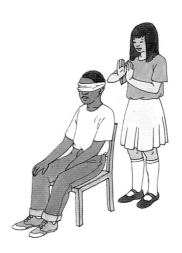

WHICH DIRECTION?
You tell where sounds come from because you have two ears, and sound waves coming from the side reach one ear before they reach the other. Your brain works out this tiny time difference and tells you the direction the sound is coming from.

Sounds coming from a source directly in front of you, or directly behind you, reach the ears at the same time. Try this test with a blindfolded, seated friend (above). Move directly behind them, quietly, then clap your hands. They will not be able to tell whether you are behind or in front of them.

HIGH OR LOW, LOUD OR SOFT
The cochlea separates high-pitched sounds from low-pitched sounds. High-pitched sounds are detected near the oval window, and low pitched sounds near the tip of the cochlea. It can also tell the difference between loud and soft sounds: loud sounds produce bigger vibrations in the fluid inside the cochlea than soft sounds.

Oval window

Low-pitched sounds detected

High-pitched sounds detected

Cochlea

Round window   Hair cells   Medium-pitched sounds detected

45

Nose and tongue

How dull life would be if you could not smell a freshly opened rose or a home-cooked meal – or if onions and chillies, or pineapples and peaches, had no taste. Your senses of taste and smell – added to those of seeing, hearing and touch – allow you to experience your surroundings fully.

Smell and taste are linked senses. Try this test. Blindfold a friend and give him or her small pieces of different foods to see if they can be identified. Now hold your friend's nose, and repeat the experiment. Without a nose to help, it is much more difficult to identify what food you are tasting. The same thing happens when you have a bad cold and your nose is blocked.

Both nose and tongue are chemical detectors. Tiny particles that dissolve in the mucus lining the nose, or in saliva swilling over the tongue, are picked up by sensors, which relay the information to the parts of the brain where you smell and taste.

WHERE ARE THE NOSE AND TONGUE?

Both tongue and nose are found inside the head. The actual 'smelling' part of the nose is not in the fleshy part sticking out from the front of your face, but in the nasal cavity behind it. The muscular tongue is firmly attached to the bottom of the mouth.

SMELL VERSUS TASTE

Your sense of smell is at least 20 000 times more sensitive than your sense of taste. You can taste the bitterness of the flavouring quinine when it is diluted two million times in water, but you can smell skunk odour diluted 30 thousand million times in air! And while your tongue can only detect four basic tastes, your nose can distinguish over 10 000 different odours.

INSIDE THE NOSE

Touch your nostrils with a finger and the back of your throat with your tongue. Between these two points lies the nasal cavity, the place where smelling happens. The nasal cavity has two sides, one for each nostril. At the top of each is a patch, no bigger than a postage stamp, covered with cells sensitive to odours. As air is breathed in, airborne particles come into contact with the patch, called the olfactory epithelium, and are detected.

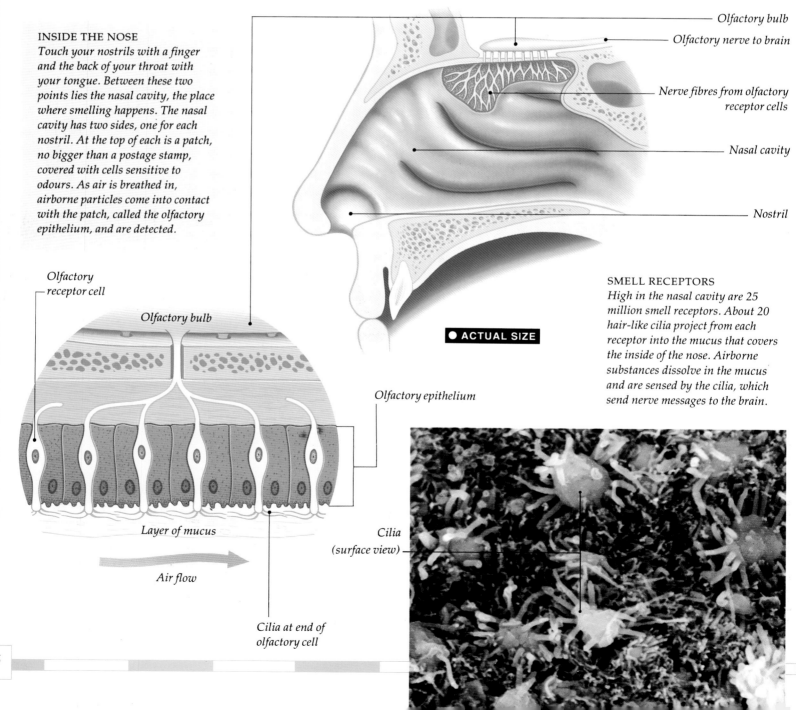

Olfactory bulb

Olfactory nerve to brain

Nerve fibres from olfactory receptor cells

Nasal cavity

Nostril

● **ACTUAL SIZE**

Olfactory
receptor cell

Olfactory bulb

Olfactory epithelium

Layer of mucus

Air flow

Cilia at end of
olfactory cell

Cilia
(surface view)

SMELL RECEPTORS

High in the nasal cavity are 25 million smell receptors. About 20 hair-like cilia project from each receptor into the mucus that covers the inside of the nose. Airborne substances dissolve in the mucus and are sensed by the cilia, which send nerve messages to the brain.

TONGUE AND TASTING

Your tongue lets you savour and enjoy your food. At the same time, it guards the entrance to the digestive system, picking out anything that may be poisonous – which is usually bitter-tasting – so that you can spit it out before it does you harm. In fact, the tongue is 8 000 times more sensitive to bitter tastes than it is to the sweet tastes that are associated with harmless and pleasant things.

The tongue's taste detectors are 10 000 microscopic taste buds. Taste buds look the same but are not all sensitive to the same tastes. And they are grouped around the tongue

in different taste areas. You can see this on the taste map.

So how can you tell the difference between so many flavours when the tongue has only four basic taste sensations? Because the brain analyses how much of the four tastes is present. It adds to this information about the temperature, texture and spiciness of food – along with the smells detected by the nose. So when you are presented with things as similar as raspberry and strawberry ice creams, for example, you are able to tell the difference without looking.

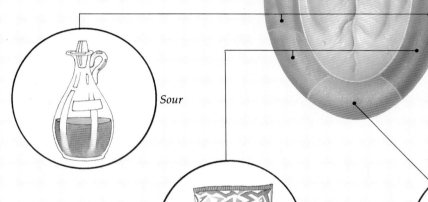

Epiglottis

Lingual tonsil

Upper surface of tongue

Sour

Salty

Sweet

Bitter

TASTE BUDS

Taste buds – the taste detectors – are too small to see. If you look at your tongue with a mirror, what you will see are hundreds of tiny bumps on the surface. These are called papillae, and make your tongue rough. The tiny taste buds line the gaps between papillae.

Papilla

Taste bud

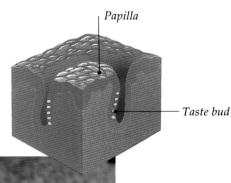

WINE TASTING

Some people's jobs depend on the fact that they can distinguish many more tastes than the rest of us. An example of this is wine tasting. Wine tasters do more than taste though. They depend on their sense of smell and their colour vision as well. First, they examine the colour of the wine. Then, they swill it around in the glass to release its smell, or 'bouquet', which they sniff. Finally, a sip of wine is swirled over the tongue and tasted. By now the tasters can tell where the wine came from, how old it is and whether it is any good.

Hormones

Consider the difference between telephoning friends for a quick chat and going round to see them for a meal. In the first case, communication is rapid and over quickly. In the second case, communication is achieved more slowly and lasts much longer.

The same comparison can be made between your nervous and hormonal (endocrine) systems. Both work together to co-ordinate the body's activities. But the nervous system does this instantly, by sending electrical impulses along the nerves, while the endocrine system takes a more leisurely approach. The endocrine glands that make up the system release over 20 kinds of chemical messengers called hormones into the bloodstream. These are carried to areas sensitive to the hormone, called target tissues, where they have a long-lasting effect.

Most endocrine glands are controlled by hormones released by the tiny pituitary gland, which is found at the base of the brain. In fact, the pituitary gland used to be called the 'conductor of the endocrine orchestra', but it is now known that it is itself controlled by part of the brain called the hypothalamus.

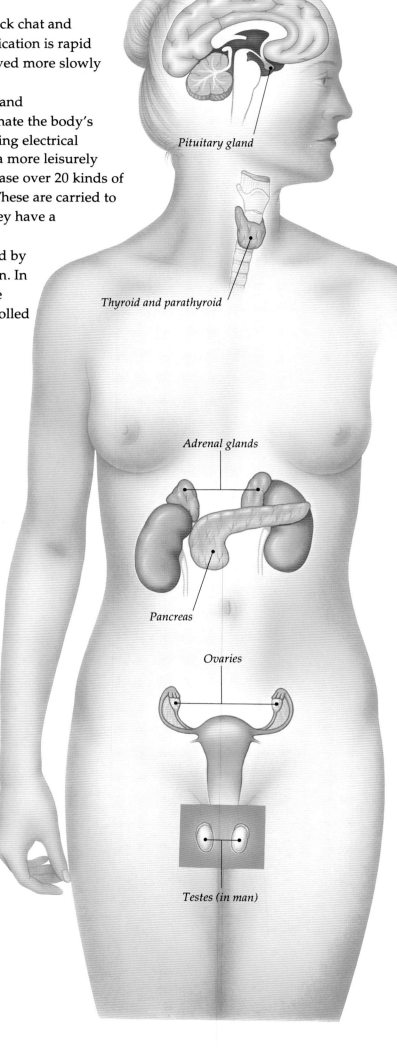

Pituitary gland

Thyroid and parathyroid

Adrenal glands

Pancreas

Ovaries

Testes (in man)

WHERE ARE THE ENDOCRINE GLANDS?

You have six main endocrine glands in your body: one in the head; two (one of which has four parts) in the chest; and three (two of which are split into pairs) in the abdomen – in males one pair, the testes, hangs outside the body.

MALE   FEMALE

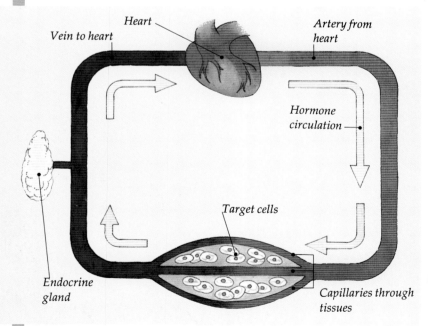

Heart

Vein to heart

Artery from heart

Hormone circulation

Target cells

Endocrine gland

Capillaries through tissues

HOW THE HORMONES WORK

A hormone has to carry its message from an endocrine gland, where it is made, to the target cells, where it has its effect. To do this, cells inside the gland release the hormone into a vein. It is then carried in the blood to the heart, which pumps it out to *the tissues, along an artery. The capillaries (see pages 20-21) then take the hormone to the target cells. And when it reaches the target cells, the hormone's molecules lock on to the surface and transmit their chemical instructions.*

PITUITARY GLAND
No bigger than a garden pea, your pituitary is the most important gland of the hormonal system. It releases hormones that control growth, stimulate the thyroid gland, tell the breasts to produce milk, trigger the contraction of the womb when giving birth, control how much urine is produced and tell the testes and ovaries to make sperm and eggs.

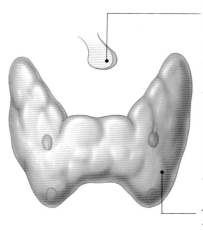

THYROID AND PARATHYROID
Your thyroid gland produces thyroxine. This controls the metabolic rate – the rate at which energy is released – of body cells. The four parathyroid glands release a hormone that controls levels of calcium in your bones and blood.

ADRENAL GLANDS
Each pyramid-shaped adrenal gland has two parts. The outer part makes over 24 hormones, including aldosterone which controls salt levels in your blood. The inner part makes the fight-or-flight hormone, adrenaline (see below right).

● ACTUAL SIZE

PANCREAS
Your pancreas produces two hormones, insulin and glucagon. Between them, they keep the level of glucose in the blood steady. Having too much, or too little, energy-providing glucose in the blood makes you very ill.

OVARIES
A woman's ovaries make the female sex hormones, oestrogen and progesterone. Oestrogen causes the development of female sexual features, such as breasts. Both hormones help regulate the menstrual cycle (see pages 52-53).

TESTES
A man's testes make the male sex hormone testosterone. Testosterone causes male sexual characteristics – such as a deeper voice, and facial and pubic hair – to develop and be maintained. Along with other hormones from the pituitary gland, testosterone stimulates the production of sperm by the testes.

GROWTH HORMONE
As its name suggests, growth hormone makes the body grow. Growth hormone is produced by the pituitary gland and has most effect on bones and muscles, making them grow longer. Its most dramatic effects can be seen during childhood and adolescence, the years when most growth takes place. Too little growth hormone during childhood causes a person to grow up to be shorter than normal. Too much growth hormone, and a person can grow to over 2.1 m (7 ft) tall.

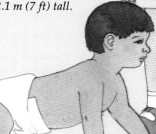

INSULIN
Insulin helps you keep a steady level of glucose in your blood, by 'telling' body cells how much glucose to take in from the blood after a meal. Without insulin, glucose levels would rise, eventually causing death. Diabetics – people who suffer from the disease diabetes – produce little or no insulin. They control their blood glucose by injecting insulin (left).

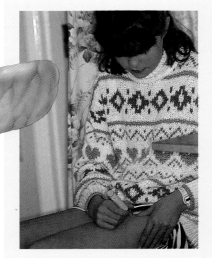

ADRENALINE
Adrenaline helps the body react if you are frightened. When you are scared, your brain sends a message to the adrenal glands, which release adrenaline into the blood. Immediately, your heart starts pounding, and you breathe more quickly. Your muscles get an increased supply of energy-providing food and oxygen so that you are ready to confront the danger – or, to run away.

Communication

Humans are the only animals that use spoken language to make themselves understood. The brain works out what you want to say, and then instructs the mouth, tongue and lips to form the words. Language is very complex. It can be used to express facts, ideas, or any number of feelings. Yet when you are not speaking, you are still busy communicating in a number of non-verbal ways, that is without using words at all.

Facial expressions can say a lot about the way you feel about yourself, and the way you relate to someone else. A real smile, or a forced one, a frown, a pout, or a grin, all serve to convey something about a person.

Keeping eye contact is important too. If you look into someone's eyes, and they return your gaze, this generally shows that you are showing interest in each other. If you stare, you indicate hostility.

Simply turning towards, or away from, someone can say much more than words, too. Gestures, body positions and movements make up the repertoire of non-verbal communication called body language.

BODY LANGUAGE

Body language is a way we communicate without words. A lot is said by the way someone holds their body, leans towards you or folds their arms. Your brain reacts to the position and movements of other people's bodies and extracts what the message of the body language might mean – perhaps this person likes you, or perhaps you bore them. So remember you may be giving away more than you think!

● ACTUAL SIZE

MAKING SOUNDS

Spoken language is a form of communication unique to humans. Your brain controls what you want to say and how you want to say it. It does this by sending messages to your larynx (voice box), tongue and lips. The larynx produces the 'raw' sounds by closing the vocal cords. These sounds are refined by the tongue to produce the 'harder' consonant sounds such as 'L' and 'S'. The production of vowel sounds – 'A', 'E', 'I', 'O' and 'U' – is controlled by the shape of your lips.

A

FACIAL MUSCLES

The muscles of your face overlay the bones of your skull, producing the features that make an individual recognizable and unique.

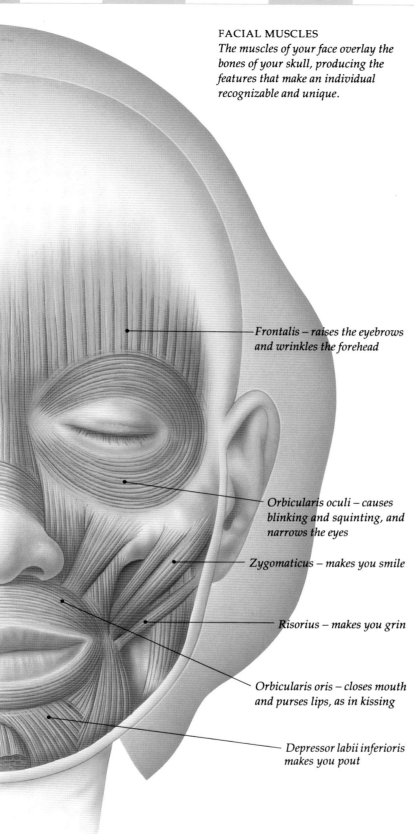

Frontalis – raises the eyebrows and wrinkles the forehead

Orbicularis oculi – causes blinking and squinting, and narrows the eyes

Zygomaticus – makes you smile

Risorius – makes you grin

Orbicularis oris – closes mouth and purses lips, as in kissing

Depressor labii inferioris makes you pout

The muscles of the face, scalp and neck pull on the skin. There are many of them and they can express a wide variety of emotions. Frowning takes more effort than smiling. You use 43 to frown but only 17 to smile.

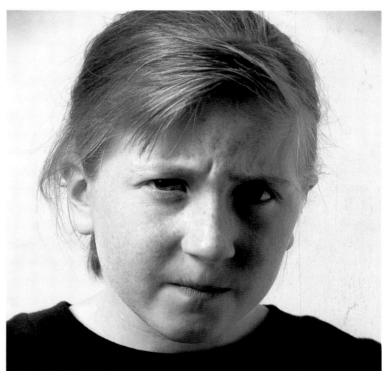

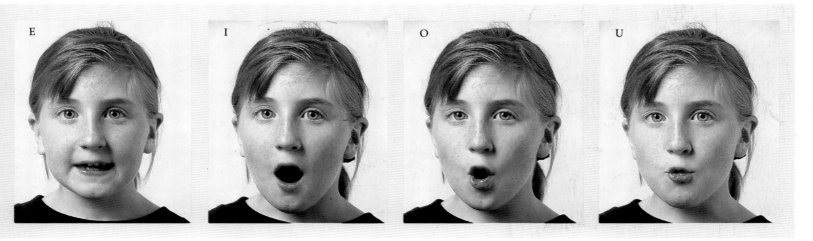

A new life

You began life as a single cell smaller than the full stop at the end of this sentence. That single cell was produced at fertilization, when chemical information from your father joined with chemical information from your mother. The result, a fertilized egg, carried all the instructions needed to make you.

Every day, millions of fertilizations take place. New human lives are starting all the time. Each depends on an encounter between a sperm – one of the tiny tadpole-like cells produced in a man's testes – and an egg, a bigger cell released each month from a woman's ovary. These two elements are united in the fertilized egg cell, which then undergoes the first of many divisions and embeds itself in the soft wall of the uterus (womb), where it continues its development for the next nine months. During that time, the single cell becomes a mass of many billions of cells which make up a new human being.

AN EGG IS RELEASED
When a girl is born, her two ovaries contain about 700 000 immature eggs. Every month, from the age of about 12 to about 50, one of these many eggs gets bigger. Then a small piece of the ovary wall splits open, and the egg is released from the ovary. This process is called ovulation. The egg is then wafted along the Fallopian tube towards the uterus. If the egg is fertilized (see below) by a sperm within the next 24 hours, it will grow into a baby in the uterus. If it is not fertilized, the egg and the lining of the uterus, which thickens to receive the fertilized egg, break down and pass out of the vagina. This is called menstruation, or having a period.

WHERE ARE THE REPRODUCTIVE ORGANS?

Most of the male reproductive system hangs outside, and towards the front of, the body, at the top of the legs. The penis and urethra also form part of the urinary system.

MALE

The female reproductive organs – the ovary, Fallopian tubes, uterus and vagina are located in the lower part of the abdomen. The vagina opens between the legs.

FEMALE

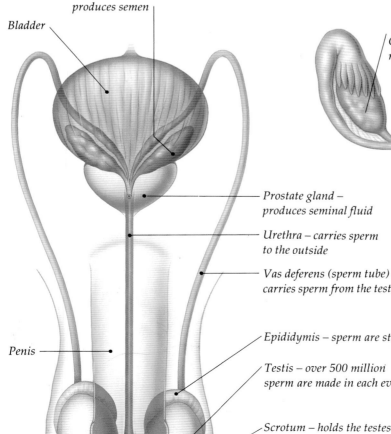

Fallopian tube

Ovary

Seminal vesicle – produces semen

Bladder

Prostate gland – produces seminal fluid

Urethra – carries sperm to the outside

Vas deferens (sperm tube) – carries sperm from the testes

Penis

Epididymis – sperm are stored here

Testis – over 500 million sperm are made in each every day

Scrotum – holds the testes outside the body

Ovary – eggs are released from here

Uterus (womb) – if the egg is fertilized, it will develop here

Fallopian tube – the egg travels along here to the uterus

Wall of uterus – thickens to receive the fertilized egg

Cervix – entrance to the uterus

Vagina – tube running from the uterus to the outside

SEXUAL INTERCOURSE

To start a new life, a sperm from the man's testes has to fertilize an egg in a woman's Fallopian tube. For this to happen, sexual intercourse, or 'making love', has to take place. Sexual intercourse is a very intimate type of contact between two people. As the couple touch and caress each other, they become sexually excited. The woman's vagina moistens. The man's penis elongates and becomes stiff. The woman then takes the penis into her vagina, and they move together.

At the height of excitement, a milky fluid called semen containing millions of sperm is squirted out of the penis and into the vagina. The sperm then begin their long journey up through the uterus and into the Fallopian tube. Here, if an egg is present, one of the few sperm which survive the journey will fertilize it.

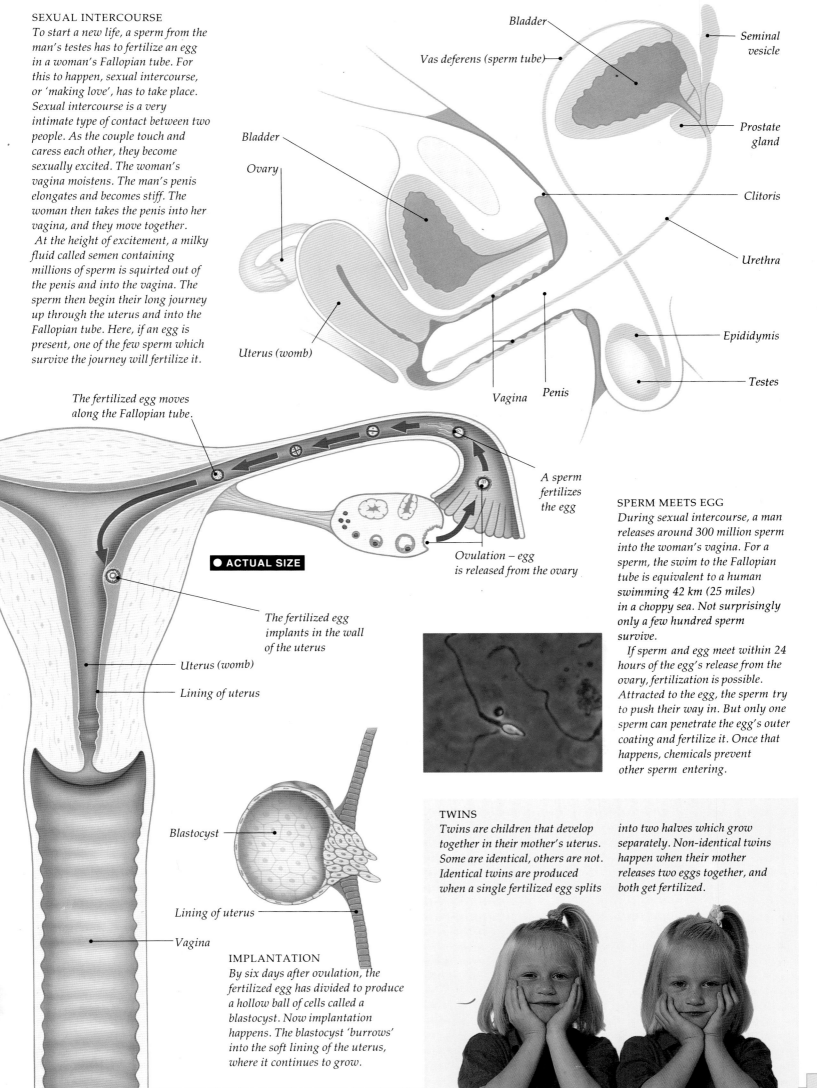

Bladder

Vas deferens (sperm tube)

Seminal vesicle

Prostate gland

Clitoris

Urethra

Epididymis

Testes

Bladder

Ovary

Uterus (womb)

Vagina

Penis

The fertilized egg moves along the Fallopian tube.

A sperm fertilizes the egg

● ACTUAL SIZE

Ovulation – egg is released from the ovary

The fertilized egg implants in the wall of the uterus

Uterus (womb)

Lining of uterus

Blastocyst

Lining of uterus

Vagina

SPERM MEETS EGG

During sexual intercourse, a man releases around 300 million sperm into the woman's vagina. For a sperm, the swim to the Fallopian tube is equivalent to a human swimming 42 km (25 miles) in a choppy sea. Not surprisingly only a few hundred sperm survive.

If sperm and egg meet within 24 hours of the egg's release from the ovary, fertilization is possible. Attracted to the egg, the sperm try to push their way in. But only one sperm can penetrate the egg's outer coating and fertilize it. Once that happens, chemicals prevent other sperm entering.

IMPLANTATION

By six days after ovulation, the fertilized egg has divided to produce a hollow ball of cells called a blastocyst. Now implantation happens. The blastocyst 'burrows' into the soft lining of the uterus, where it continues to grow.

TWINS

Twins are children that develop together in their mother's uterus. Some are identical, others are not. Identical twins are produced when a single fertilized egg splits into two halves which grow separately. Non-identical twins happen when their mother releases two eggs together, and both get fertilized.

53

In the womb

When you ask someone how old they are, they always say a number of years that dates from the day they were born. In fact, if you want to know how old someone really is you should add nine months to this figure. These are the nine months that it takes the dot-sized fertilized egg to grow inside a mother's womb into a fully-developed baby.

The fertilized egg divides repeatedly and grows into a tiny embryo. By five weeks, the heart is beating. By eight weeks, the embryo looks human and is now called a foetus. Day by day, during the following seven months, the foetus grows rapidly until, nine months after fertilization, it is ready to be born. Throughout its development, the foetus floats inside a protective bag of liquid, kept at a constant temperature inside the womb. Food and oxygen are carried to the foetus along the umbilical cord that links it to the mother.

MULTIPLYING CELLS

A new life begins when a father's sperm meets a mother's egg at fertilization (see pages 52-53). Thirty-six hours after fertilization, the fertilized egg has moved further towards the uterus, and has divided into two. By 72 hours, three more divisions have happened to produce a ball of 16 cells called a morula. By 144 hours, further cell divisions have produced a hollow ball of cells called a blastocyst, which attaches itself to the wall of the uterus. Within eight weeks, this will be recognizable as a tiny human being.

Two cell stage – 1½ days after fertilization

Morula stage – 3 days after fertilization

Blastocyst stage – 6 days after fertilization

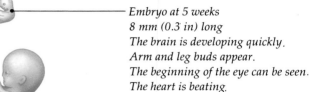

Embryo at 5 weeks
8 mm (0.3 in) long
The brain is developing quickly. Arm and leg buds appear. The beginning of the eye can be seen. The heart is beating.

Foetus at 8 weeks
3 cm (1.25 in) long
The main outside parts of the body are now formed: ears, eyes, mouth, arms, legs, fingers and toes.

Foetus at 12 weeks
9 cm (3.75 in) long
All the internal organs are formed. Sex can now be determined.

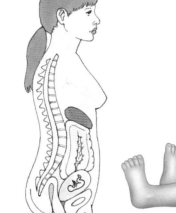

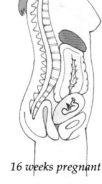

Before pregnancy

16 weeks pregnant

Foetus at 16 weeks
14 cm (5.5 in) long
Face looks human. Sucking movements of lips and blinking occur.

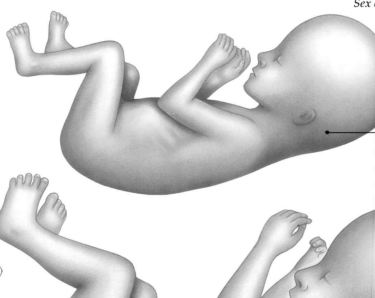

28 weeks pregnant

38 weeks pregnant

Foetus at 20 weeks
19 cm (7.5 in) long
Hair grows on the head and body. Kicking and hiccuping can be felt by the mother.

THE GROWING UTERUS

Before pregnancy, the uterus is the size of a fist. By 16 weeks it fills the space inside the hips, and the mother's abdomen starts to bulge. By 28 weeks, it fills about half the abdomen, and by the end of pregnancy, at 38 weeks, the uterus fills most of the abdomen, right up to the ribs.

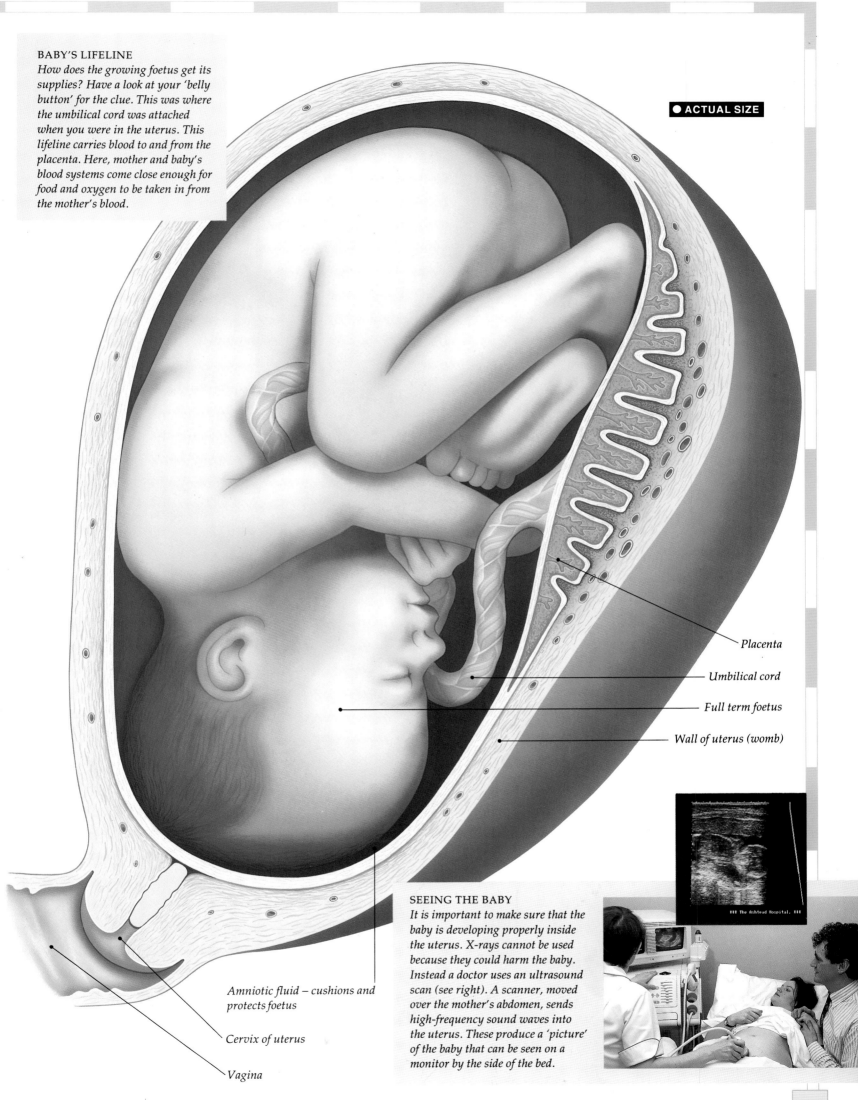

BABY'S LIFELINE
How does the growing foetus get its supplies? Have a look at your 'belly button' for the clue. This was where the umbilical cord was attached when you were in the uterus. This lifeline carries blood to and from the placenta. Here, mother and baby's blood systems come close enough for food and oxygen to be taken in from the mother's blood.

● ACTUAL SIZE

Placenta

Umbilical cord

Full term foetus

Wall of uterus (womb)

Amniotic fluid – cushions and protects foetus

Cervix of uterus

Vagina

SEEING THE BABY
It is important to make sure that the baby is developing properly inside the uterus. X-rays cannot be used because they could harm the baby. Instead a doctor uses an ultrasound scan (see right). A scanner, moved over the mother's abdomen, sends high-frequency sound waves into the uterus. These produce a 'picture' of the baby that can be seen on a monitor by the side of the bed.

Birthday

About 266 days after fertilization, a baby is fully developed and ready to emerge into the outside world. The baby signals to its mother that it is ready to be born. She realizes the baby is on its way because of the pains she feels in her uterus, caused by the contractions of the muscles that will push the baby out of her body.

Birth can take anything between two hours and 24 hours or more. On average, babies weigh 3.4 kilograms (7.5 pounds), and are about 50 centimetres (20 inches) long. When the baby appears, the first thing it does is to expand its lungs and start breathing. It is no longer cocooned within a safe, warm environment. Suddenly, it senses light and sounds around it, feels the air on its skin and notices the change in temperature. It feels hungry and instinctively seeks out its mother's breast for its first feed. For the first few years the child needs constant attention. It will be years before it becomes independent.

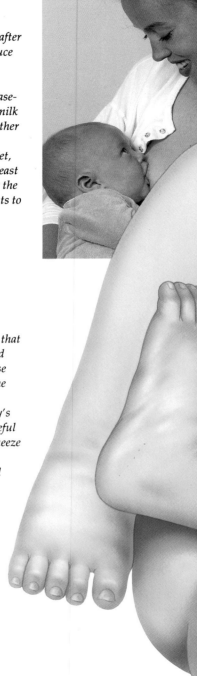

BREAST-FEEDING
Many mothers breast-feed their babies for the first months of their lives. Breast milk is better for the baby than dried milk because it is fresh, free from germs, and contains the food the baby needs in the correct proportions.

For the first two or three days after birth, however, the breasts produce not milk, but a yellowish liquid called colostrum. This is rich in body-building proteins and disease-fighting antibodies. When true milk production starts, the baby's mother releases around 1 litre (nearly 2 pints) of bluish-white, quite sweet, milk each day. Sucking at the breast is an automatic, reflex action for the baby. It also stimulates the breasts to make more milk.

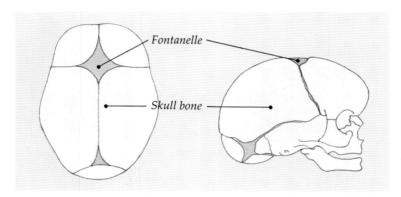

Fontanelle

Skull bone

A FLEXIBLE SKULL
Your brain is surrounded and protected by a number of bones that are fused together to form a solid skull. But in a baby's skull, these bones are not fused together. The gaps between them are called fontanelles. This makes the baby's skull slightly squashable – a useful feature when its head has to squeeze through the narrow gap in the centre of its mother's pelvis and down the vagina.

THE STAGES OF LABOUR
Labour is a series of events during which the baby is pushed out of its mother's uterus. When labour begins (1), the uterus starts to contract, weakly at first, then more strongly and more frequently. The cervix, the opening to the uterus, gets wider, and the bag of fluid surrounding the baby bursts – this is called 'breaking the waters'. This stage of labour can last for 12 hours, or even longer.

The uterus then starts contracting strongly every 2 or 3 minutes. The

uterus muscles push the baby's head out through the vagina (2). Once the head – the baby's widest part – has appeared, the rest of the body is delivered more easily (3). This stage takes between 20 and 50 minutes.

Once the baby is born and starts to breathe (4), the umbilical cord that links it to its mother is clamped and cut. About 30 minutes later, the placenta – now called the afterbirth – is delivered and the mother can relax after many hours of labour.

1. BEGINNING OF LABOUR

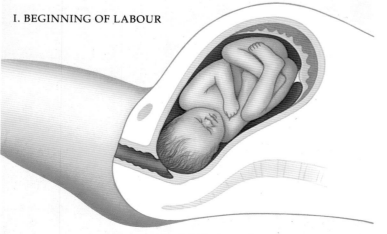

2. HEAD ABOUT TO EMERGE

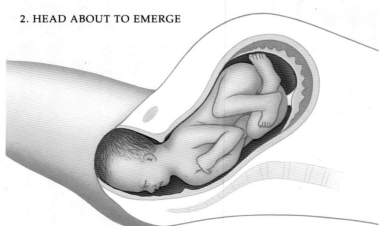

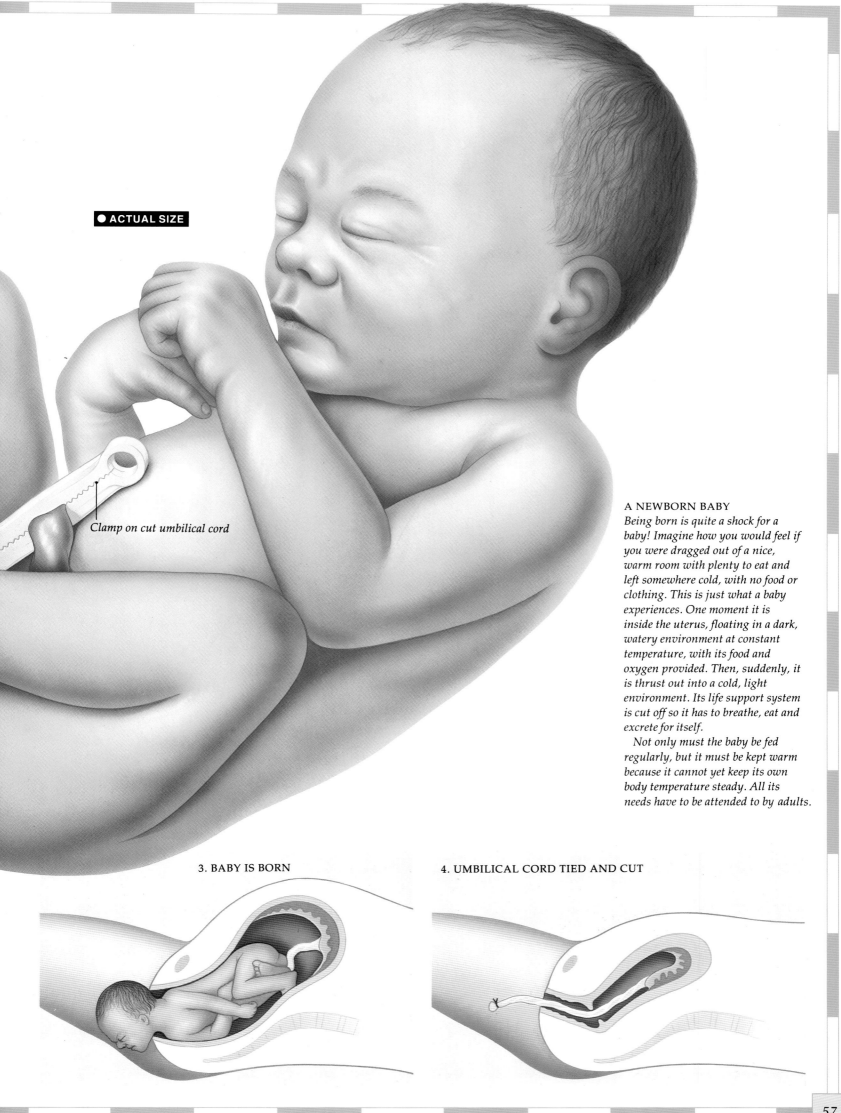

● ACTUAL SIZE

Clamp on cut umbilical cord

A NEWBORN BABY

Being born is quite a shock for a baby! Imagine how you would feel if you were dragged out of a nice, warm room with plenty to eat and left somewhere cold, with no food or clothing. This is just what a baby experiences. One moment it is inside the uterus, floating in a dark, watery environment at constant temperature, with its food and oxygen provided. Then, suddenly, it is thrust out into a cold, light environment. Its life support system is cut off so it has to breathe, eat and excrete for itself.

Not only must the baby be fed regularly, but it must be kept warm because it cannot yet keep its own body temperature steady. All its needs have to be attended to by adults.

3. BABY IS BORN

4. UMBILICAL CORD TIED AND CUT

The growing body

Look at some photographs of yourself when you were a baby. The proportions of your body were different. As a baby, your head was about one-quarter the length of your body. By the time you are grown up, your head will be only about one-eighth your body's length.

Your body grows, changing shape and size, through childhood right up to the age of 20. But it does not grow at the same rate during those years. Growth is very rapid during the first year of life. In middle childhood, the growth rate slows, then it suddenly increases again for the growth spurt that happens in girls between the ages of 10 and 14, and in boys between the ages of 12 and 16. This is the time of puberty, when the child's body matures and becomes adult.

After the age of 20, the body does not change much outwardly, although inside body cells are constantly being replaced. In old age, growth is actually 'reversed', and the body shrinks a little.

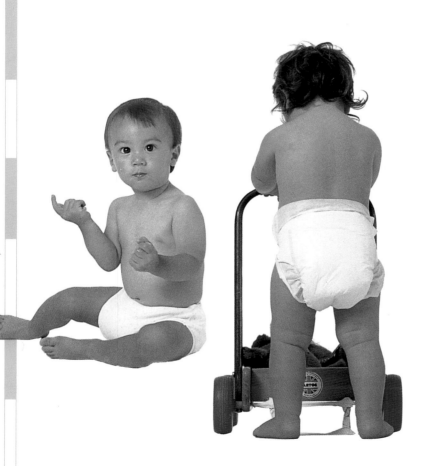

EARLY CHANGES IN THE BODY

Great changes happen to boys' and girls' bodies during the first year of life. Weight triples and height increases by a half. The brain grows from a quarter to a half adult size. The arms and legs grow faster as well, so that the head is no longer as large in proportion to the rest of the body. And the first teeth appear.

The first movements a baby makes are automatic reflex movements, such as grasping and

sucking. Most have disappeared by the end of three months, as the baby starts to learn movements of its own. First, it learns to control its upper arms and legs, then its hands and feet, and finally its fingers. By nine months it can hold its head steady and crawl on its hands and knees. By the time it is one, the infant starts to walk and can pick up objects between fingers and thumb, and hand them to an adult if asked.

INFANT

6 months
The average height is 0.66 m (26 in), and average weight 7.5 kg (16.5 lb). Boys are slightly taller and heavier than girls. The baby can sit on a chair and reach for objects, or pass a toy from hand to hand.

1 year
The average height is 0.75 m (2 ft 5½ in), and average weight 10 kg (22 lb). Boys are slightly taller and heavier than girls. The infant can pull itself up by holding on to furniture, and is learning to walk.

CHILD

6 years
The average height is 1.17 m (3 ft 10 in), and average weight 21.6 kg (47.5 lb). Boys are slightly taller and heavier than girls. The child can walk and talk, read and write and is able to match similar objects.

8 years
The average height is 1.3 m (4 ft 3 in), and average weight 26.8 kg (59 lb). Boys are slightly heavier and taller than girls. The child's reading and writing powers have improved, and it can now ride a bicycle.

CHANGES DURING PUBERTY

Puberty marks the time when girls' and boys' bodies mature, at the end of childhood and the beginning of adulthood. The body grows rapidly and changes happen inside it that enable it to produce children of its own.

Puberty starts earlier in girls than boys, between the ages of 10 and 14, and lasts between two-and-a-half and three years. As the girl's body gets taller and heavier, her hips widen and more fat gets laid down under her skin, producing the more 'rounded' shape of an adult woman. The girl's breasts grow and her nipples enlarge and stick out more.

Hair grows in her armpits and around her genitals. Her uterus and vagina enlarge and her ovaries start releasing eggs each month, as menstruation begins.

In boys, puberty starts between the ages of 12 and 16 and takes around four years to complete. As his body gets heavier and taller, a boy's shoulders widen and his muscles thicken. Hair grows on his face, armpits and chest, and around his genitals. The boy's penis and testes get bigger, and the testes start producing sperms. His larynx (voice box) also enlarges, and his voice breaks and gets deeper.

ADOLESCENT

12 years
The average height is 1.5 m (4 ft 11 in) for boys, and 1.52 m (5 ft) for girls. The average weight is 38.2 kg (84 lb) for boys, and 40 kg (88 lb) for girls. Girls are taller and heavier because their puberty growth spurt starts earlier.

14 years
The average height is 1.63 m (5 ft 4 in) for boys and 1.60 m (5 ft 3 in) for girls. The average weight is 48.6 kg (107 lb) for boys and 49.1 kg (108 lb) for girls. Boys have now caught up with girls in terms of height, but not weight.

ADULT

By the age of 18, girls are generally fully grown, whereas boys will carry on growing for another couple of years. Boys are taller and heavier than girls. Boys' average height is 1.75 m (5 ft 9 in), and their average weight is 65 kg (143 lb). The girls' average height is 1.63 m (5 ft 4 in), and their average weight is 54.6 kg (120 lb).

By now, individuals are developing an adult sense of identity, and forming more mature relationships with people of their own age and with their parents. And they are able to have children of their own.

Glossary

A

ABDOMEN the part of the body between the diaphragm and the hips. The abdomen contains the stomach, intestines, kidneys and bladder.

ABSORPTION taking digested food into the bloodstream through the wall of the small intestine.

ADRENAL GLAND one of two glands that produce many hormones, including adrenaline, and are found on top of each kidney.

ANTIBODY a chemical produced by lymphocytes that helps destroy invading disease-causing organisms.

ANUS the lower end of the digestive system, through which undigested food is pushed out.

AORTA the body's largest artery, which carries blood from the heart to the body.

ARTERY a blood vessel that carries blood away from the heart.

ATRIUM one of two atria, the upper chambers of the heart.

B

BACTERIA a group of very simple, one-celled organisms. Some types cause diseases such as pneumonia and typhoid in humans.

BILE a liquid produced in the liver, stored in the gall bladder, and released into the small intestine to help digest fats.

BLADDER a muscular, elastic bag that stores urine produced by the kidneys until it is ready for release.

BLOOD a liquid tissue that circulates around the body in tubes called blood vessels. It consists of a liquid part, plasma, in which red and white blood cells are suspended.

BONE a piece of supporting tissue that consists of collagen fibres, to give it elasticity, and mineral salts, such as calcium, to give it hardness.

C

CANINE a type of tooth used for gripping and tearing food.

CAPILLARY the smallest type of blood vessel. Millions of capillaries carry blood to, and from, all the body's cells.

CARBON DIOXIDE a kind of gas found in the air. We breathe out more carbon dioxide than we breathe in because it is released during respiration inside all cells.

CARTILAGE a flexible structural tissue found, for example, covering the ends of bones in joints, and supporting the ear and nose.

CELL one of the millions of basic building blocks that makes up the human body, and the bodies of all other organisms.

CENTRAL NERVOUS SYSTEM (CNS) the brain and the spinal cord.

CEREBELLUM the part of the brain that produces smooth, co-ordinated movements.

CEREBRUM the largest part of the brain. It is responsible for thought, language, learning, memory and personality.

COCHLEA a snail-shaped, coiled tube in the inner part of the ear that contains sound receptors.

CONES cells found in the retina of the eye that are sensitive to coloured light.

CONNECTIVE TISSUE a type of tissue that supports organs and forms tendons and ligaments.

D

DEOXYRIBONUCLEIC ACID (DNA) the substance found in all cells that carries a person's genetic information.

DERMIS the inner part of the skin, below the epidermis. It contains blood capillaries and nerve endings.

DIAPHRAGM the muscle sheet that separates the chest (or thorax) from the abdomen. The diaphragm plays an important role in breathing.

DIGESTION the process of breaking down large food molecules into smaller food molecules that can then be absorbed into the bloodstream by the body.

E

ELECTROCARDIOGRAM (ECG) a record, in the form of a graph, of the electrical activity of the heart.

EMBRYO the name given to a developing baby up to the end of its eighth week inside the uterus.

ENDOCRINE GLAND a gland that produces hormones.

ENZYME a substance that speeds up chemical reactions. Digestive enzymes speed up the breakdown of food during digestion.

EPIDERMIS the outer part of the skin, above the dermis.

EPIGLOTTIS a flap at the back of the throat that covers the entrance to the windpipe during swallowing.

F

FERTILIZATION the joining together of a sperm and egg.

FOETUS the name given to a developing baby between its eighth week in the uterus and its birth.

G

GALL BLADDER a small bag behind the liver in which bile is stored prior to release into the small intestine.

GLAND an organ specialized to produce a substance either for further use inside the body (e.g. a salivary gland producing saliva) or for elimination (e.g. a sweat gland producing sweat).

H

HAEMOGLOBIN an orange substance found inside red blood cells that carries oxygen.

HEART the four-chambered muscular pump that pushes blood around the body.

HORMONE a chemical 'messenger' released into the blood by an endocrine gland to cause a change elsewhere in the body.

I

INCISOR a type of tooth used for biting off chunks of food.

INTESTINE the long tubular section of the digestive system that fills most of the abdomen. In the small intestine, the first and longer section, food is digested and absorbed. The shorter large intestine carries waste to the outside.

IRIS the coloured part of the eye that surrounds, and controls the size of, the pupil.

J

JOINT the place where two or more bones meet.

K

KIDNEY one of two organs found in the upper abdomen that remove waste from the blood and produce urine.

L

LARYNX the organ that lies between the throat and windpipe and produces sounds.

LIGAMENT the tough tissue that holds bones together at joints.

LIVER a large organ, found in the abdomen, in which hundreds of chemical processes take place, many linked to digestion.

LUMEN the cavity inside a blood vessel or other type of tube inside the body.

LUNGS the spongy organs found inside the chest in which oxygen is exchanged for carbon dioxide.

LYMPH excess fluid draining into the tissues from blood capillaries and carried away by the lymph system.

LYMPH NODE one of many small organs in the lymph system that filters disease-causing organisms out of the lymph.

LYMPHOCYTE a type of white blood cell that produces antibodies.

M

MENSTRUATION the breakdown and loss of the lining of the uterus each month that occurs if an egg has not been fertilized.

MOLAR a type of tooth used for crushing and chewing food.

MONOCYTE a type of white blood cell that eats bacteria and other foreign bodies.

MUCUS a slimy secretion produced by various parts of the body including nose and mouth.

MUSCLE a type of tissue that can contract, or get shorter.

N

NEPHRON one of millions of filtration units that remove waste from blood flowing through the kidneys.

NERVE a long cylindrical tissue that carries nerve impulses to and from the central nervous system.

NEURONE a nerve cell. A nerve is made up of many neurones.

NEUTROPHIL a type of white blood cell that eats bacteria and other foreign bodies.

O

OESOPHAGUS the part of the digestive system that carries food from the mouth to the stomach.

ORGAN a collection of tissues that work together to carry out a particular function; for example, the kidney.

ORGANELLE a microscopic structure inside a cell that carries out a particular function.

OSSICLES the three tiny bones in the middle ear that carry sounds from the outer ear to the cochlea.

OVARY a female sex organ in which eggs and sex hormones are produced.

OXYGEN a kind of gas. Oxygen is breathed in and used by body cells to release energy from food molecules during respiration.

P

PALATE the roof of the mouth.

PANCREAS a gland found below the stomach that produces hormones, and enzymes involved in digestion.

PHARYNX the muscular tube that links the nose and mouth to the windpipe and oesophagus.

PITUITARY GLAND a tiny pea-sized gland found below the brain that produces hormones that control many other hormone-producing glands inside the body.

PLACENTA the organ that links a developing foetus to its mother.

PLASMA the liquid part of blood in which blood cells are suspended.

PLATELET a cell fragment found in blood that plays an important part in clotting.

PREMOLAR a type of tooth used for crushing and chewing food.

PULSE the rhythmic expansion of an artery that happens with each heart beat. A pulse can be felt where the artery passes over a bone.

PUPIL the black hole in the front of the eye through which light enters.

R

RESPIRATION the process occurring inside all body cells by which oxygen is used to release energy from fuel molecules such as glucose. Carbon dioxide is released as waste, and is breathed out.

RETINA the light-sensitive layer that covers the inside of the eye. Nerve fibres from the retina carry impulses to the brain.

RODS cells found in the retina of the eye that are sensitive to dim light.

S

SALIVA a liquid involved in digestion that is produced by salivary glands surrounding the mouth.

SEMICIRCULAR CANALS a part of the inner ear that enables us to balance.

SKELETON the bones of the body that together support it. Some bones also protect delicate organs such as the brain, lungs and heart.

SPERM a male reproductive cell, produced in the testes. A sperm fuses with the female egg during fertilization.

SPHINCTER a ring of muscle that controls flow of liquid through a system. An example is the pyloric sphincter that controls the flow of food from the stomach into the small intestine.

SPINAL CORD the part of the central nervous system that links the brain with the rest of the body.

STOMACH a part of the digestive system in the form of a muscular bag that lies between the oesophagus and the small intestine.

SYSTEM a collection of organs that work together to carry out a particular function; for example, the digestive system.

T

TASTE BUD one of many thousands of tiny structures in the tongue that detects flavours.

TENDON A tough, inelastic band of fibres that links a muscle to a bone.

TESTIS one of two male sex organs in which sperm and sex hormones are produced.

THORAX the part of the body between neck and diaphragm. The thorax contains the lungs and heart.

TISSUE a collection of similar cells that performs a particular function; for example, muscle tissue.

TRACHEA the tube, surrounded and strengthened by rings of cartilage, that carries air from the throat to the lungs.

U

UREA a waste substance produced in the liver, and excreted from the body, in the urine, by the kidneys.

URINE a waste fluid produced by the kidneys. It consists mainly of water, but also contains dissolved wastes including urea.

UTERUS a hollow, thick-walled organ that is part of the female reproductive system in which an embryo develops.

V

VALVE a structure found inside veins and the heart that stops blood flowing backwards and ensures that it flows around the body in one direction only.

VEIN a type of blood vessel that carries blood towards the heart.

VENA CAVA the body's largest vein, which carries blood from the body to the heart.

VENTRICLE one of the two lower chambers of the heart.

VOCAL CORDS two folds of tissue in the larynx that are moved and stretched to produce sounds.

Index

Acknowledgements

Quarto would like to thank the following for providing photographs, and for granting permission to reproduce copyright material:

Barts Medical Illustration: 25br; Roger Chester:Bubbles: 27al; Mike Evans:Life File: 50bl; Eye Ubiquitous:TRIP: 47br; Jacqui Farrow:Bubbles: 17cl, 17bl, 17bc, 27bcr, 31ar, 56ar; Carol Fulton:Bubbles: 55br; Andrew Gasson: 42ar; Brian Gibbs:TRIP: 45ar; Institute of Laryngology & Otology Photographic Department: 26cl, 46br; Martin Jackson:Bubbles: 36br; Brian Lake:TRIP: 13bl, 41ca; National Medical Slide Bank: 18c, 19bl, 22br, 23al, 52ar, 53ar; NASA:TRIP: 36ac; Oxford Scientific Films: 13al, 13ar, 13br, 18cr, 18bc, 18br, 31br, 36ar, 37cl, 38cl, 40ar, 40cl, 41al, 41bl, 47bl; Claire Paxton:Bubbles: 27bl; Quarto: 6, 7; H.C.Robinson:Bubbles: 49ar; Helene Rogers:TRIP: 10ar, 10cl, 10bl, 10br, 18cl, 23bc, 27ar, 27bcl, 29al, 29ar, 29bl, 29br, 35al, 41ra, 41rc, 41rb, 41c, 49br, 55ar; Frans Rombout:Bubbles: 23cr, 53br; David Simson:das PHOTO: 25ar; J.M.Steinlein:Bubbles: 36bc; Loisjoy Thurston:Bubbles: 21bl, 30ar, 31cr, 36cr; TRIP: 10cr, 15ar, 36cl; Flora Torrance:TRIP: 24bc, 44bl; Bob Turner:TRIP: 10al; Ian West:Bubbles: 19al, 27br, 28ar, 28bl, 41cb; Jennie Woodcock:Bubbles: 17al, 36bl.

(a = above, b = below, c = centre, l = left, r = right)

While every effort has been made to trace and acknowledge all copyright holders, we would like to apologize should any omissions have been made.